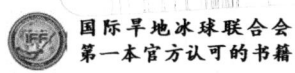

国际旱地冰球联合会
第一本官方认可的书籍

北欧时尚运动——旱地冰球
Nordic Fashion Sport Floorball

主　编：陈　新
　　　　王　骏
副主编：韩殿秀

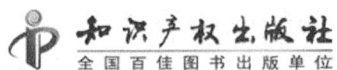

知识产权出版社
全国百佳图书出版单位

内容提要

旱地冰球运动 20 世纪 70 年代中期在瑞典问世,世界上第一个国家旱地冰球联盟(SIBF)于 1981 年成立。目前,旱地冰球运动正在向欧洲以外的亚洲、澳洲以及美洲传播,至今已有 50 多个国家开展这个项目。国际旱地冰球联合会(IFF)总部在芬兰,每年组织各种不同的世界大赛,包括男子、女子世界杯,世界大学生比赛,等等。旱地冰球随处可开展、简单易学、老少皆宜,诸多魅力使得这个运动在世界各国飞速的发展起来。

2007 年,旱地冰球运动进入中国,深受大学生们的喜爱,为了使大家更好的了解并学习旱地冰球运动,本书对旱地冰球运动的历史、发展、技术、战术、赛事、规则进行了细致的分析与讲解。

本书可作为推广旱地冰球运动的教材使用。

责任编辑:荆成恭

图书在版编目(CIP)数据

北欧时尚运动——旱地冰球/陈新,王骏主编.
—北京:知识产权出版社,2012.9
ISBN 978-7-5130-1471-7

Ⅰ.①北… Ⅱ.①陈…②王… Ⅲ.①冰球运动—教材 Ⅳ.①G862.3

中国版本图书馆 CIP 数据核字(2012)第 197387 号

北欧时尚运动——旱地冰球
BEIOU SHISHANG YUNDONG HANDI BINGQIU

陈 新 王 骏 主编 韩殿秀 副主编

出版发行:	知识产权出版社			
社 址:	北京市海淀区马甸南村 1 号	邮 编:	100088	
网 址:	http://www.ipph.cn	邮 箱:	bjb@cnipr.com	
发行电话:	010-82000860 转 8104/8102	传 真:	010-82000860 转 8353	
责编电话:	010-82000860 转 8341	责编邮箱:	jingchenggong@cnipr.com	
印 刷:	北京九州迅驰传媒文化有限公司	经 销:	新华书店及相关销售网点	
开 本:	880mm×1230mm 1/32	印 张:	9.5	
版 次:	2012 年 12 月第 1 版	印 次:	2019 年 5 月第 3 次印刷	
字 数:	185 千字	定 价:	38.00 元	

ISBN 978-7-5130-1471-7/G·511(4337)

出版权专有 侵权必究

如有印装质量问题,本社负责调换。

Preface

This book is a comprehensive manual designated for readers to start playing floorball in your school, your club, your city or your country. It demonstrates the technique and tactics on how to get started and guides readers, step by step, to establish a team or an organization, to get people involved as well as to win the challenges.It will hopefully be a handy guidance for creating the best environment for the sport.

前　言

　　本书旨在给读者们提供广泛综合的素材，指导大家在自己的学校、俱乐部、城市或国家开始旱地冰球运动。本书展示了启动本运动的技巧和方法，一步一步引领大家明晰如何吸引更多人广泛参与、如何建团设组、如何应对挑战并赢得胜利。本书有望帮助大家创建最好的运动氛围和环境。

IFF Vision （IFF寄语）

International Floorball Federation has for a number of years tried to find a good cooperative partner in China, in order to develop and promote the sport.

With the help of Mrs. Chen Xin, IFF has found a trustworthy partner in Shanghai International Studies University, and we believe that the activities made in China will help to spread the sport to more schools in the country, and will help to build a stronger presence for Floorball in China.

We have great hopes for the development of Floorball in China and I hope to see the development of a university series and in the long run also the presence of a national team in the IFF competitions.

IFF would like to congratulate Mrs. Chen Xin for the efforts made to put this book together and the work done to promote Floorball in China.

We are quite sure that the book will help promote and popularize the sport in China.

IFF Secretary General : John Liljelund

目 录
Contents

第一章　旱地冰球运动概述 …………………… 1
Chapter One　Overview of Floorball …………… 1
　　第一节　旱地冰球运动起源与发展简介 ……… 1
　　Section One: The Origin and Development of Floorball … 1
　　第二节　旱地冰球的特点 ……………………… 8
　　Section Two : The Characteristics of Floorball ………… 8
　　第三节　旱地冰球的发展态势 ………………… 12
　　Section three: The Development Tendency of Floorball   12

第二章　旱地冰球运动的基本技术战术 ………… 14
Chapter Two　The Basic Techniques and Tactics of Floorball ………………………………… 14
　　第一节　旱地冰球技术介绍 …………………… 14
　　Section One: The Introduction of Floorball Techniques … 14
　　第二节　旱地冰球的战术介绍 ………………… 36
　　Section Two: The Introduction of Floorball Tactics ……… 36

第三章　无处不在的旱地冰球运动 ……………… 43
Chapter Three　Floorball Game is Everywhere ……… 43
　　第一节　街头旱地冰球 ………………………… 43
　　Section One: Street Floorball ……………………………… 43

I

第二节 沙上旱地冰球和沼泽旱地冰球 …… 47
Section Two: Sand Floorball and Swamp Floorball …… 47

第三节 青少年旱地冰球 …… 50
Section Three: Youth Floorball …… 50

第四节 公司里的旱地冰球 …… 68
Section Four: Floorball in Companies …… 68

第四章 旱地冰球运动的综合技术 …… 70
Chapter Four The Basic Technique of Floorball …… 70

第一节 综合技术的练习 …… 71
Section One: The Training of Basic Technique …… 71

第二节 比赛战术认识 …… 170
Section Two: The Comprehension of Match Tactics … 170

第五章 旱地冰球重大赛事 …… 172
Chapter Five Important Floorball Events …… 172

第六章 旱地冰球竞赛规则 …… 178
Chapter Six The Rules for Game …… 178

第一节 比赛场地 …… 179
Section One: Rink …… 179

第二节 比赛时间 …… 184
Section Two: The Game …… 184

第三节 参赛人员 …… 192
Section Three: Participants …… 192

第四节 装备 …… 198
Section Four: Equipment …… 198

第五节　定位球 206
Section Five: Fixed Situations 206

第六节　处罚 232
Section Six: Penalties 232

第七节　得分 267
Section Seven: Goals 267

第八节　裁判手势 273
Section Eight: Consequence Signs 273

第九节　犯规手势 278
Section Nine: Offence Signs 278

第十节　场地规格 291
Section Ten: Illustration of the Rink 291

附录
专业旱地冰球运动词汇汉英对照表 292

Appendix
Vocabulary of Professional Floorball Terms in Chinese & English 292

参考资料及来源 295
References or Sources 295

参考书目和作者 296
References & Authors 296

第一章 旱地冰球运动概述
Chapter One　Overview of Floorball

Section One: The Origin and Development of Floorball

第一节　旱地冰球运动起源与发展简介

Origin

Some roots of Floorball (Also Floorhockey) can be dated as early as 1958. The idea of plastic sticks (with both shaft and blade) was born in a plastic industry in Lake-ville, Minneapolis, USA. They introduced sticks and other plastic material under the name Cosom. Cosom floorhockey has grown afterwards in both USA and Canada. Since then many game series have been played in North America and Canada, but mainly for children and youth. One of the biggest tournaments, Floorhockey Tournament, was

起源

旱地冰球（Floorball音译"福乐球"，也称Floorhockey）最早起源于1958年，美国明尼阿波利斯市的一家塑料厂生产出塑料球杆（包括杆和击球板）。他们用Cosom作为品牌名字推销其球杆和其他塑料产品。后来美国和加拿大开始了Cosom的地板曲棍球（Floorhockey）运动。虽然此后北美和加拿大举办了多年系列比赛，但主要是为儿童和青少年而设。作为最大的锦标赛之

北欧时尚运动——旱地冰球
Nordic Fashion Sport FLOORBALL

arranged for the first time in the beginning of the1960s in Battle Creek Michigan.

The first Cosom plastic stick was introduced to Sweden in 1968 and after that a lot of different versions of games with balls and pucks were played in Sweden. In the middle of the 1970s, the idea of trying to establish ONE sport was formed on the Cosom material and with influence from basketball and ice hockey. The first national floorball federation in the world, SIBF (Svenska Innebandy Forbundet—Swedish Floorball Federation)was founded in 1981 in Sweden. The first official rulebook was marketed in

一，地板曲棍球锦标赛首次在20世纪60年代初于密歇根州巴特尔克里克市举行。

Cosom塑料球杆于1968年传入瑞典，此后，形式多样的球类和冰球运动在瑞典开始流行。20世纪70年代中期，受篮球及冰球的影响，人们开始有了在Cosom的设备基础上创立一项专门运动的想法。世界上第一个国家旱地冰球联盟（SIBF）于1981年在瑞典成立。1983年，第一本官方规则手册问世。1985年，瑞典旱地冰球

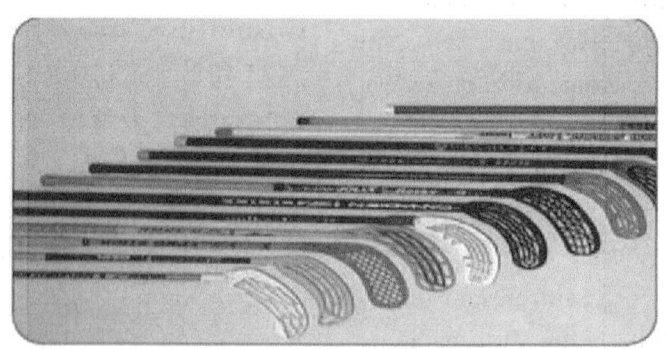

Floorball Sticks from the 80's picture from FFF

第一章 旱地冰球运动概述
Chapter One   Overview of Floorball

1983. The Swedish Floorball Federation (SFF) became a member of the National Sports Confederation in 1985.

International Development

To establish a federation with only Sweden and Finland did not seem appropriate, so a search for other countries with floorball begun, and a version of floorball in Switzerland

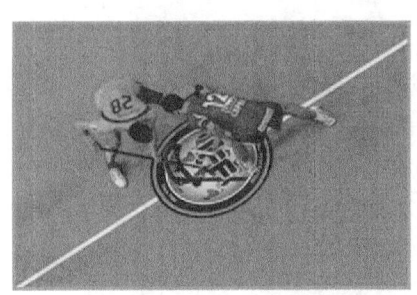

was found. Sweden, Finland and Switzerland established the International Floorball Federation (IFF) on the 12th of April 1986 in Huskvarna, Sweden. IFF is an ordinary member of General Association of International

联盟（SFF）成为瑞典国家体育联盟会员。

国际发展

联盟只有瑞典和芬兰两个国家不是很合适，所以人们开始争取其他国家加入旱地冰球运动，在瑞士也出现了旱地冰球的一种形式。

1986年4月12日，瑞典、芬兰和瑞士在瑞典的胡斯克瓦纳（Huskvarna）市成立了国际旱地冰球联盟（IFF），该联盟（IFF）是国际单项体育联合会总会（GAISF）

北欧时尚运动——旱地冰球
Nordic Fashion Sport FLOORBALL

Sports Federations (GAISF), a full member of International Olympic Committee (IOC) and cooperates with both International University Sports Federation (FISU) and E-Sports Management Australia (EMSA).

IFF now stresses three different fields, namely, marketing, development and politics in the field of sports.

的普通会员,国际奥林匹克委员会(IOC)的正式会员,并与世界大学生运动联合会(FISU)及澳大利亚电子竞技运动管理局(EMSA)合作。

IFF目前致力于三个领域的运作:旱地冰球运动的市场营销、发展和策略。

第一章　旱地冰球运动概述
Chapter One　Overview of Floorball

Fast Growing

Floorball becomes the fastest growing sport in Czech Republic, Finland, Norway, Sweden and Switzerland.

Floorball is now globally spread to Europe, Asia, Australia and America.

It is to be established in several countries such as Germany and the USA.

Number of licensed players among sports gives top five ranking in Sweden, Finland, Czech Republic and Switzerland.

Floorball is moving more and more into central Europe, Asia and the Pacific.

发展迅猛

旱地冰球运动在捷克、芬兰、挪威、瑞典和瑞士发展十分迅猛。

目前，旱地冰球正在向欧洲、亚洲、澳洲以及美洲传播。

德国、美国等国也在积极开展此项运动。

在瑞典、芬兰、捷克以及瑞士，拥有旱地冰球IFF证书的运动员数量居所有运动项目前五位。

旱地冰球现在日益快速传向中欧、亚洲及环太平洋地区。

北欧时尚运动——旱地冰球
Nordic Fashion Sport FLOORBALL

Floorball As A Worldwide Sport

作为国际运动的旱地冰球

Floorball is now played in following countries:

开展旱地冰球运动的国家如下：

Argentina, Armenia, Australia, Austria, Belarus, Belgium, Brazil, Canada, Czech Republic, Denmark, Estonia, Finland, France, Georgia, Germany, Great Britain, Hungary, Iceland, India, Indonesia, Iran, Ireland, Israel, Italy, Japan, Latvia, Liechtenstein, Lithuania, Malaysia, Moldova, Mongolia, Netherlands, New Zealand, Norway, Pakistan, Philippines, Poland, Portugal, Romania,

阿根廷、亚美尼亚、澳大利亚、奥地利、白俄罗斯、比利时、巴西、加拿大、捷克共和国、丹麦、爱沙尼亚、芬兰、法国、格鲁吉亚、德国、英国、匈牙利、冰岛、印度、印度尼西亚、伊朗、爱尔兰、以色列、意大利、日本、拉脱维亚、列支敦士登、立陶宛、马来西亚、摩尔多瓦、蒙古国、荷兰、新西兰、挪威、

第一章 旱地冰球运动概述
Chapter One Overview of Floorball

Russia, Serbia, Sierra Leone, Singapore, Slovakia, Slovenia, South-Korea, Spain, Sweden, Switzerland, Thailand, Turkey, Ukraine, USA.

巴基斯坦、菲律宾、波兰、葡萄牙、罗马尼亚、俄罗斯、塞尔维亚、塞拉利昂、新加坡、斯洛伐克、斯洛文尼亚、韩国、西班牙、瑞典、瑞士、泰国、土耳其、乌克兰、美国。

IFF Member Associations   IFF会员国

Argentina, Armenia, Australia, Austria, Belarus, Belgium, Brazil, Canada, Czech Republic, Denmark, Estonia, Finland, France, Georgia, Germany, Great Britain, Hungary, Iceland, India, Indonesia, Iran, Ireland, Italy, Israel, Japan, Latvia, Liechtenstein, Lithuania, Malaysia, Moldova, Mongolia, Netherlands, New Zealand, Norway, Pakistan, Philippines, Poland, Portugal, Romania, Russia, Serbia, Singapore, Slovakia, Slovenia, South Korea, Spain, Sweden, Switzerland, Thailand, Turkey, Ukraine, USA.

阿根廷、亚米尼亚、澳大利亚、奥地利、白俄罗斯、比利时、巴西、加拿大、捷克共和国、丹麦、爱沙尼亚、芬兰、法国、格鲁吉亚、德国、英国、匈牙利、冰岛、印度、印度尼西亚、伊朗、爱尔兰、意大利、以色列、日本、拉脱维亚、列支敦士登、立陶宛、马来西亚、摩尔多瓦、蒙古国、荷兰、新西兰、挪威、巴基斯坦、菲律宾、波兰、葡萄牙、罗马尼亚、俄罗斯、塞尔维亚、新加坡、斯洛伐克、斯洛文尼亚、韩国、西班牙、瑞典、瑞士、泰国、土耳其、乌克兰、美国。

北欧时尚运动——旱地冰球
Nordic Fashion Sport FLOORBALL

Section Two: The Characteristics of Floorball

Easy to learn, easy to start and inexpensive to run. A new generation among sporting youth.

• Very strong penetration among the 12-19 year olds.

• Very strong participation of girls and women.

• One of the few sports which is equal between genders.

第二节　旱地冰球的特点

易学，易上手，成本低。新生代中兴起的运动。

• 12-19岁的年轻人参与度很高；

• 女性参与度很高；

• 少数几个提倡男女平等参与的运动项目之一。

第一章 旱地冰球运动概述
Chapter One Overview of Floorball

Due to the rapid growth of the sport and the lower level of media exposure, floorball has built a very strong internal information structure.

• Over 300 000 unique users per month.

• Over 600 000 sessions per month.

• Easy to enter a well-organized sports community.

• Very strong presence in the schools.

• Direct contact to nearly 300 000 players.

• Growing media exposure.

鉴于旱地冰球运动发展迅猛而媒体曝光率低，旱地冰球建构了强劲的内部信息架构。

• 每月30万以上个体参与者；

• 每月60万人次的集会；

• 加入组织完善的运动共同体便捷；

• 形成校园亮点；

• 与近30万运动人士直接联系；

• 日益增多的媒体宣传。

北欧时尚运动——旱地冰球
Nordic Fashion Sport FLOORBALL

Easy to learn, but difficult to master.

入门易,打好难。

Easy to learn, and also fun to play.

入门易,乐趣多。

Young sport in a fast growing phase.

飞速发展的新项目。

Challenging attitude vs. traditional sport.

相比传统运动更富挑战性。

• Entertaining and spectator friendly.

• 娱乐性强,观众喜爱;

• Lots of interactions, actions and goals during a game.

• 比赛中颇多互动、行进和进球。

第一章 旱地冰球运动概述
Chapter One Overview of Floorball

Floorball has brought a group of alternative people, compared to traditional sports lovers.

• They are young rebels of traditional sports.

• They have their own culture, which is achieved by themselves.

The new blood:

• They are dynamic.

• Full of energy.

• Being happy and relaxed.

The advantages of Floorball:

• Cost to start is reasonable, and the threshold to begin playing Floorball is low.

• It suits both boys and girls.

• It is interesting and consists of new blood.

• It is a young sport developing rapidly.

• It is expected to be played in more countries.

• It has great potential for growth.

相对传统体育爱好者,旱地冰球带来"另类"人群。

• 是传统运动中年轻的"叛逆者";

• 依托自身,营造自己的文化。

作为新鲜血液,他们:

• 活力充沛;

• 激情四射;

• 快乐轻松。

旱地冰球的优点:

• 项目启动费用合理,运动入门门槛低;

• 男孩、女孩都适合;

• 趣味性强,融新鲜血液;

• 项目年轻,增长速度快;

• 有望在更多的国家开展;

• 很大的发展潜力。

Section Three: The Development Tendency of Floorball

Today floorball is a very popular sport around the world. The number of players and teams are increasing every year and there is no sign that the development would stop.

　　Floorball is an invasive sport officially played with five players and a goal keeper on each side. It has similarities with both field hockey and ice hockey but also some similarities with other team ball sports. It is played with a plastic stick and a plastic hollow ball, with holes.

　　Floorball is the sport of today and is becoming the universal sport of tomorrow. During the 25 years, the development and growth of the sport has been amazing. Since the first Floorball Federation was founded in 1981 in Sweden, the sport has spread all over the world and it is

第三节　旱地冰球的发展态势

　　目前，旱地冰球运动在世界各地深受欢迎，团队和队员数量逐年增长，而且这种增长态势丝毫没有停止的迹象。

　　旱地冰球运动进攻性强，正规打法双方各有五名场地队员和一名守门员。它与曲棍球和冰球都有相同点，也与其他团队球类运动有相似之处。本运动使用一根塑料球杆和一个表面有孔的空心塑料球。

　　旱地冰球发展飞速，大有今天刚开始，明天就普遍流行的态势。25年来，旱地冰球的发展和成长速度不可思议。自1981年首个旱地冰球联合会于瑞典成立以来，这项运动开始在世界范围内普及，目前已有60多个国家

第一章 旱地冰球运动概述
Chapter One Overview of Floorball

now played in over 60 countries.

Due to the great variability of the game, floorball can be played almost anywhere, with a varied number of players on the field. Floorball is a fascinating sport with a lot of speed and excitement.

One of the reasons behind the popularity of floorball is the easiness to start playing: no specific skills are needed in the beginning and the rules are simple, you just need sport shoes, a stick and ball. Floorball can be played as a fitness sport where equality between the genders is well realized.

Mixed Floorball has been played since the early stages of the sport. In addition to school children and students, today many workplace and special interest groups have also taken up floorball, and the so called intercompany matches have come to stay.

开展这项运动。

这项运动相当灵活,几乎可以在任何地方进行,场地球员的数量也是可变的。旱地冰球运动充满了速度和激情,十分吸引人。

旱地冰球之所以深受欢迎,原因之一就是这项运动极易开展:开始时不需要特定的技巧,规则简单易懂,你只需要一双运动鞋,一个球杆和球。旱地冰球也可作为一种健康运动,男女享有平等地位。

这项运动的早期阶段就已经有男女混合赛了。除了校园内的孩子和学生,现在许多工作场所及专门的兴趣小组都开展了旱地冰球运动,而且也出现了公司间的交流赛。

第二章 旱地冰球运动的基本技术战术
Chapter Two The Basic Techniques and Tactics of Floorball

Section One: The Introduction of Floorball Technique

第一节 旱地冰球技术介绍

Stance, running with a ball, pass, receiving the pass, shoot, protecting the ball, dribbling/faking.

站位，带球，传球，接球，射门，护球，运球/假动作。

1.Stance

1.站位

1)Holding the stick with two hands, upper hand covering the whole upper end.

1) 双手握杆，上面的手抓住整个杆顶上端；

2)The lower hand at least 20 cm from the upper hand.

2) 下方的手距离上方的手至少20厘米；

3)Centre of gravity low with bent knees and straight back.

3) 双膝弯曲，后背挺直，降低身体重心；

4) Blade on the floor.

4) 击球板放于地板上；

第二章　旱地冰球运动的基本技术战术
Chapter Two　The Basic Techniques and Tactics of Floorball

5) Legs shoulder width apart with one foot slightly forward.

5) 两腿分开与肩齐宽，一只脚略微靠前；

6) Keeping a balanced stance.

6) 站位保持平衡；

7) The length of the shaft being an important factor when choosing a stick.

7) 选择球杆，长度是重要因素。

2.Running with a ball

2.带球

1) The ball touches the blade all the time.

1) 球一直接触击球板；

2) Light touch not hitting.

2) 轻触，不能击打；

3) Be ready to pass from back and forehead.

3) 准备好正手或后手传球；

4) Protect the ball.

4) 保护好球。

·15·

3.Pass

The right pass stance is a side-on position feet alongside each other slightly apart with knees bent.

Keep a balanced stance.

Head up all the time to see the field.

Keep the ball close to the blade.

The blade should always point in the direction of the pass afterwards.

3.传球

正确的传球站位是侧站，双脚并排，双膝分开，微微弯曲；

站立姿势保持平衡；

保持抬头姿势，关注场地；

击球板始终靠近球；

传球后，击球板应始终朝向传球方向。

第二章 旱地冰球运动的基本技术战术
Chapter Two　The Basic Techniques and Tactics of Floorball

Forehand pass

Grip:

Steady two handed grip with the lower hand close to the lower edge of the grip.

Execution:

1) The pass starts with the ball behind the body.

2) keep the ball close to the blade.

3) The blade is drawn from behind towards the target with increasing speed.

4) The ball is released from the blade before it has passed the front foot.

5) The longer the trail of the blade from behind, the more precise the passing.

6) The blade should always point in the direction of the pass afterwards.

正手传球

握杆:

　　始终保持双手握杆，下面的手握杆时位于球杆的下半部分。

动作要领:

　　1) 传球动作从球在身后时就开始；

　　2) 击球板始终靠近球；

　　3) 击球板从后面以加速度击向目标；

　　4) 球未过前脚时，即离杆传出；

　　5) 击球板从身后拖的距离越长，传球越准；

　　6) 传球后，击球板应始终朝向传球方向；

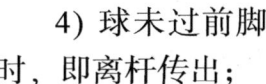

7)The blade should be pressed on the floor to avoid bounces.

8)A very forceful pass with enough rotation in the upper body, and with right amount of drag from behind the body, the pass is more accurate.

When:

Used for example after faking a shot or after the player has dribbled the ball using body protection.

Short forehand pass

Grip:

Same as previous.

Execution:

1)This method of pass is faster.

2)The touch of the ball is very short.

3)There still exists some flexibilities of touching the ball.

4)The ball is released from the blade without following through on the level of the front foot.

7) 击球板要压在地板上以防反弹；

8) 上身转体充分，身体后部适当拉伸，传球更加有力也更加精准。

适用于：

例如：假动作射门之后或者以身体掩护运球之后可以使用正手传球。

短正手传球

握杆：

与正手传球握杆姿势相同。

动作要领：

1) 这种传球速度更快；

2) 触球时间很短；

3) 在触球中依然有一些灵活性；

4) 触球板无需和前脚达同一个水平线，即可将球击出；

第二章 旱地冰球运动的基本技术战术
Chapter Two The Basic Techniques and Tactics of Floorball

5) The right action should cause the ball leave the blade quickly and the ball doesn't rebound when rolling.

6) The ball is hit too much in front, or the angle of the blade is too big, the ball will go up in the air.

5) 操作正确，球会很快离开击球板，且滚动过程中不会反弹；

6) 如果击球板击球的位置太过靠前或者击球板的角度过大，球就会被打到空中。

When:

The pass is fast and accurate, and can be executed from almost any position in small and tight situations.

Long backhand pass

Grip:

The grip is two handed, but hands are closer together than in forehand pass.

Execution:

1) When receiving a pass with a backhand, cushion as in forehand pass.

适用于：

传球速度很快且要求精准时，这种传球在小区域或者防守严密的情况下几乎可以在任何位置使用。

长后手传球

握杆：

双手握杆，长后手传球比正手传球时双手距离近。

动作要领：

1) 接反手传球和接正手传球相同，都要注意缓冲；

第二章 旱地冰球运动的基本技术战术
Chapter Two The Basic Techniques and Tactics of Floorball

2) Passing with a long back drive with the blade touching the ball all the time.

2）长后手传球时，击球板始终触球；

3) Rotation in the upper body should be followed through.

3）传球瞬间，上半身随之转动。

When:

适用于：

Backhand pass is used when passing from forehand side is obstructed by the opponent.

正手传球路线被对方球员切断时可以使用反手传球。

Aerial (a high ball)

空中传球（高球）

Grip:

握杆：

The grip as in previous techniques.

与前面讲到的正规握杆方法相同。

北欧时尚运动——旱地冰球
Nordic Fashion Sport FLOORBALL

Execution:

1)In aerial passes the touch with the ball is crucial and the height of the pass is determined by the angle of the blade.

2)The ball is passed slightly in front of the front foot.

3)The speed of the hit is determined by the backswing.

4)The blade slides along the surface in a straight line towards the ball.

5)The blade is angled back the moment it strikes the ball.

动作要领：

1) 对空中传球而言，触球点很关键，而传球的高度则取决于球拍的角度；

2) 球在前脚的前方轻轻传出；

3) 击球的速度取决于向后挥拍的速度；

4) 击球板滑过地面沿着一条直线击向球；

5) 击球瞬间，击球板应回倾。

第二章 旱地冰球运动的基本技术战术
Chapter Two The Basic Techniques and Tactics of Floorball

When:

An aerial pass is appropriate when a player needs to clear the pressure from the defensive zone or more controlled pass when the opponent has covered the space with a stick and the pass needs to be lifted up in the air, for example 2 versus 1 situations.

Short backhand pass

Grip:

Same as previous, but also one handed grip possible.

Execution:

1) Passing with backhand is a quick slight hitting.

2) The blade shouldn't touch the floor but the ball.

3) The speed of the blade is controlled by a short backswing.

适用于:

当进攻球员需要排除来自防守区域的压力,或者当对方球员用球杆将传球路线切断时要将球控制好并从空中传出,需要使用高空传球,譬如2对1时。

短后手传球

握杆:

短后手传球的握杆方法与长后手握杆方法相同,不过也可以单手握杆。

动作要领:

1) 后手传球为快速轻击;

2) 击球板不能碰地板,只能碰球;

3) 击球的速度取决于反手挥拍的速度。

When:

Backhand pass is used when passing from forehand side is obstructed by the opponent.

One hand pass

Grip:

Grip with only upper hand used.

Execution:

1) A short backswing used before hitting the ball with either back or forehand side depending on the situation.

2) The blade should not be lifted higher than knee level.

When:

Hit/direct a loose ball into the right direction or out of opponent's reach or after dribbling with one hand used. Gives a better reach to the player and saves

适用于:

若正手传球路线被对方球员切断时可以使用反手传球。

单手传球

握杆:

一只手上部握杆。

动作要领:

1) 击球板击球之前要有一个回拉球杆的动作,根据场上情况使用反手或者正手传球;

2) 击球板的高度不得超过膝盖。

适用于:

单手运球之后,用来将一个没有控制好的球打到或调整到正确的方位或者使对方无法接触到球。如果球员没有时间控球时单手传球可以将球传好并且能够节省时

第二章　旱地冰球运动的基本技术战术
Chapter Two　The Basic Techniques and Tactics of Floorball

time when the player does not have time to take control of the ball. Used by more experienced players.

间。有经验的球员单手传球用的比较多。

4.Receiving the pass

4.接球

Grip:

Same as previous.

握杆:

与正规握杆姿势要求相同。

Execution:

1)Blade on the floor.

2)Balanced stance.

3)The basic stance is the same as passing, and tilt even much.

4)Keep your head up all the time to see the field.

5)Try to touch the ball as smoothly as you can with flexible hands.

6)Cushion is the most important thing while receiving a pass.

7) Both stick and body can be used to receive or control a pass, both these methods must be trained frequently.

动作要领:

1) 击球板放在地板上;

2) 保持站立姿势平衡;

3) 基本的站立姿势和传球一样,侧身多一点;

4) 始终抬头关注场地;

5) 接球要流畅,手要柔和、灵活;

6) 接球的时候缓冲非常关键;

7) 球杆和身体都可以用来接球或控制球,两种方法都需要经常性训练;

8)The ball should be received with the blade (waiting for the ball close to the front foot) and then moving the blade backwards when making contact with the ball (soft hands) – this will stop the ball from hitting the blade and bouncing away from the

8）必须使用击球板接球（击球板靠近前脚等待来球），接球时击球板向后回带起到缓冲作用（用力要轻）——这可以防止球在打到击球板的时候再次反弹，因此能让球员立刻将球控制好；

第二章　旱地冰球运动的基本技术战术
Chapter Two　The Basic Techniques and Tactics of Floorball

blade again therefore giving the player immediate control.

9) The ball should be received in front of the body.

10) Receiving aerial passes demands good ball handling skills.

11) Also the body can be used to capture an aerial pass (chest, thighs and feet).

12) Receiving the ball correctly might open gaps in defense and create scoring chances.

5. Shoot

Drag Shoot

Grip:

Same as in passing forehand.

Execution:

1) The opposite side's foot in front, weight is on the back foot.

2) The blade has a long back drive along the surface and the ball is released on the level of the front foot.

9) 接球动作应该在身体前方完成；

10) 接高球的时候需要很好的控球技术；

11) 身体也可以用来接高球（胸、大腿以及脚）；

12) 准确接球可能会打破防守或创造得分机会。

5. 射门

长射

握杆:

和正手传球握杆姿势相同。

动作要领:

1) 反手侧的脚在前，身体重心落在后脚上；

2) 击球板要从身体后方有一段拖长的距离，当球与前脚水平后才离杆传出；

•27•

3) In the end of the shot, the blade should be pointing towards the goal, and the weight should be transferred totally to the front foot.

When:

When a player has time to aim and shoot, usually forwards from the side (especially from rotation).

Pros:

Accurate.

Cons:

The back drive takes a long time to execute.

wrist shot

Grip:

Same as above.

Execution:

1) Chest should be towards the goal, also the same side's foot in front as the shooting side.

3) 射门结束后，击球板要指向球门方向，身体重心要完全转移至前脚。

适用于：

当球员有时间瞄准并射门时，通常是在身体侧前方传出（尤其在转体时传出）。

优点：

射门精确。

局限：

拖杆的过程花费时间长。

腕射

握杆：

与一般射门握杆姿势相同。

动作要领：

1) 身体必须朝向球门，射门侧与持杆侧一致，该脚在前；

Chapter Two　The Basic Techniques and Tactics of Floorball

2) The ball is released from the blade close to the foot in front.

3) The ball touches the blade in a very short time (short shot by forehand).

4) Shot by wrist when moving.

When:

A player has gained position close to the goal, straight from a pass.

Pros:

Accurate and fast, can be shot from even bad positions, goalkeeper has less time to react than in other shots.

2) 球接近前脚后时即可离杆传出；

3) 球接触击球板时间很短（正手短射）；

4) 移动中使用腕射。

适用于：

当球员的位置靠近球门，能够直接接球时。

优点：

射门精确并且快速，即使位置不佳也可以射门，与其他射门方式相比，守门员更难及时做出反应。

Cons:

Player has to be close to the goal.

Forehand drive

Grip:

Hands closer to each other than in the wrist shot.

Execution:

1) The opposite side's foot in front to gain the rotation of the upper body, at the time of the shot the ball should be in front of the body, and slightly to the side.

2) The ball shouldn't be as close to the body as in wrist shot.

3) The ball is hit with the blade's heel, so that the ball is lifted up in the air.

4) The backswing might look a bit like in golf.

5) Can also be shot with a shorter back swing when the shot is not as hard but maybe a bit more accurate.

局限：

球员必须靠近球门。

正手大力射门

握杆：

与腕射相比，正手大力射门两手更近。

动作要领：

1) 反手一侧脚在前以推动上身转体，击球的瞬间球要在身体前方，稍离体侧；

2) 球不能像在腕射的时候那样靠近身体；

3) 使用击球板的根部击球，使得球被击向空中；

4) 向后挥拍的方式与打高尔夫有些类似；

5) 力量不需要太大，但可能更精确时，向后挥拍的距离可以缩短。

第二章　旱地冰球运动的基本技术战术
Chapter Two　The Basic Techniques and Tactics of Floorball

When:

A player has time to take the shot, mostly used by defenders from the middle zone.

Pros:

Good long distance shot when there are players screening the goalkeeper.

Cons:

The back swing takes time.

Slap shot

Grip:

Wider grip similar to wrist shot grip.

Execution:

1) The opposite side's foot in front than the shooting side, wide stance, weight on the front foot.

2) The back swing should be quite long but the stick shouldn't exceed the waist level.

3) Just before hitting the ball the blade should touch the floor

适用于:

当球员有时间射门时，多为防守球员在中场的时候使用。

优点:

当有队员挡住守门员视线时，正手大力射门是不错的选择。

局限:

挥拍需要时间。

抽射

握杆:

与腕射的握杆姿势相同，两手距离要宽一些。

动作要领:

1) 反手侧脚位于正手侧脚前，双脚距宽，重心在前脚上；

2) 挥拍距离要足够长，但球杆不能超过腰部；

3) 临近击球时，击球板接触地面，且射门后击球板

and the blade should be pointing towards the goal in the end of the shot.

When:

The player has time to prepare for the shot, also defenders from the middle zone.

Pros:

Hard and unpredictable, especially when there is a player screening the goalie.

Cons:

Takes time to shoot.

Backhand shot

Grip:

Hands close to each other.

Execution:

1)Foot in front is on the same side with shoulder, usually facing the goal.

2)Can also be executed with back facing the goal.

3)The blade touches the ball on the level of the front foot, or

必须指向球门。

适用于:

当球员有足够的时间准备射门，且防守一方球员在中场的时候。

优点:

射门力量大且防不胜防，尤其是当有球员挡住守门员视线时。

局限:

射门需要的时间长。

反手射门

握杆:

双手靠近。

动作要领:

1) 前脚与身体同一侧的肩部方向一致，通常面对球门；

2) 背对球门的时候也可以采用；

3) 触球点和前脚在同一

第二章 旱地冰球运动的基本技术战术
Chapter Two　The Basic Techniques and Tactics of Floorball

slightly in front of it.

When:

When the player does not have the position to shoot from forehand side, or if the opponent has blocked the forehand side.

Pros:

Unpredictable for the goalkeeper, especially when only one hand is used, can also be shot with back facing the goal.

Cons:

Player has to be close to the goal, usually shoot from very short distance.

个水平线上，或稍稍靠前。

适用于:

当球员所处的位置不适合采用正手射门时，或者对方球员封锁了正手射门的路线时。

优点:

守门员无法预料，尤其是用一只手射门时，背对球门时也能采用。

局限:

球员必须离球门很近，通常射门的距离很短。

6. Protecting the ball

1) Player has a balanced stance.

2) Use your body, feet and hands to protect the ball.

3) The blade should cover the opponents side of the ball.

4) Good control of the ball.

Use your body to protect the ball

1) Keep your body between the ball and the opponents.

2) Keep the ball as far from the opponents as possible.

3) Keep a low stance and keep your head up.

Use the stick to protect the ball

1) Keep distance from the

6.护球

1) 球员保持平衡的站立姿势；

2) 用身体、脚和手护球；

3) 击球板应该护住靠近对手的球侧；

4) 控好球。

用身体护球

1) 将身体档在球和对手之间；

2) 使球离尽量远离对方球员；

3) 保持低的比赛站位，抬头注视赛场。

用球杆护球

1) 运球时尽量远离对手；

第二章 旱地冰球运动的基本技术战术
Chapter Two The Basic Techniques and Tactics of Floorball

opponents when dribbling.

2) Dribble with two hands clasping the stick when the ball is away from your body.

3) Use the blade to protect the ball.

7. Dribbling/Faking

1) The ball should stay close to the blade.

2) Grip should be two handed (when dribbling on backhand side, a one hand grip can be used.)

3) Develop your ball handling skills as good as you can.

4) Speed and body control should be practiced and developed.

5) Try to move the defender to the direction you want.

6) Quick movement, sudden change of speed and direction are crucial.

7) The opponent should be tricked into moving in a certain direction with a false cue such as an eye contact to a team mate.

2) 当球离开身体时，双手一起握拍运球；

3) 用击球板护球。

7. 运球/假动作

1) 保持球在击球板附近；

2) 必须双手握杆（反手运球时可以使用单手握杆）；

3) 尽力提高持球技术；

4) 加强训练，提高速度和身体控制能力；

5) 尽量让对手按照你希望的方向移动；

6) 快速移动，突然变速，疾速转向；

7) 假动作（如与队友进行误导眼神交流）将防守球员虚晃向错误的方向移动；

8) A false shot maybe executed to get past the opponent.

8) 射门的假动作便于有效过人。

Section Two: The Introduction of Floorball Tactics

第二节　旱地冰球的战术介绍

The floorball tactics have a strong effect on the game. The floorball tactics consists partly of individual tactics and partly of team tactics.

旱地冰球的战术对比赛结果影响显著，分为个人战术和球队战术。

1.Individual tactics

1.个人战术

A player's profile is made up by technical and physical abilities together with game sense. Game

队员的素质取决于他的个人技术、身体技能和对赛场判断力。赛场判断力包括

第二章 旱地冰球运动的基本技术战术
Chapter Two　The Basic Techniques and Tactics of Floorball

sense consists of understanding the game, reading the game and decision making. Reading the present game situation and predicting the next action help the player to make the best decision depending on the position they are in. Individual tactics are best learned with the help of game situation roles.

2.Game situation roles

The ball carrier has three options. First aim is to score, therefore to shoot. The second option is to pass to a player who has even a better chance to shoot. The third option a ball carrier has is to dribble the ball into a better position to shoot or pass. This demands reaction speed and the ability to read the game. Even though the ball carrier has the responsibility to make the decision, the non-ball carriers also have the responsibility to assist him/her by screening, creating space and passing lanes etc. Inside the game, all the roles and duties interact. They all

队员对比赛的理解、赛场上的察觉能力和及时决断的能力。正确把握赛场上的情况并准确预计下一步行动可以帮助队员在自己的位置上做出正确的决策。就赛场情况球员担当不同角色，有助于个人技术达到最佳水平。

2.赛场球员位置

带球队员有三个选择：首要目的是得分，因此他可以选择射门；第二个选择是将球传给有更好射门机会的队员；第三是将球运至一个更好的位置以便射门或传球。这就需要球员具备极快的反应速度以及对场上情况的把握能力。带球队员有义务做出及时的判断，无球队员同样也需要通过掩护、创造空档或者交叉跑位等方式来帮助他/她进行射门或者传球。赛场上，所有位置和职责都互动，这些都考验球员对空间、速度、方向和时

demand the player's ability to estimate space, speed, direction and time. It must be understood however, that the roles switch very quickly during a game and a player is in a respective role only for a short period of time. With junior players these individual tactics should not be emphasized as they are shown in the textbook. This would probably end up with total confusion, so the roles and the duties should be introduced gradually in the progression with the development of the game sense.

Also the ability to outplay the opponent by transferring the situations from two against two to two against one, or even two against zero, is crucial. By creating zone power plays, (2 against 1, 3 against 2 or vice versa in a small area) helps the defending team to steal the ball from the opponent, and on the offensive side, it always creates a better scoring possibility.

间的评判能力。需要注意的是，赛场上不同球员之间的位置转换是很快进行的，球员各自的位置也只持续很短的一段时间。对于技术尚不熟练的队员，这些个人战术不需要像在教材中所展示的内容那样着重强调，否则可能会造成球员训练的混乱。因此角色和职责的内容应当在球员对比赛的把握能力不断提高的过程中慢慢渗透。

将2对2的局面转换至2对1甚至是2对0的局面也是战胜对方至关重要的战术。通过制造区域优势战术（如2对1、3对2，小范围内反之亦可）有助于防守一方从对方手中将球断下；对于进攻方，有助于创造更好的得分机会。

第二章　旱地冰球运动的基本技术战术
Chapter Two　The Basic Techniques and Tactics of Floorball

3. Team tactics

Team tactics is the team's tactical play system that the team uses in order to gain order and discipline in its play, as well as provide safe ways to act in given situations for the players. When five players are on the court at the same time, they should know what to do in different situations, and with given tactics, it is easier to make them aware of team mate's next actions.

Team tactics are also important for the coach to bring out the best in each player. Determining positions according to each player's capacities, whether it's physical or mental, is the best way of utilizing the recourses.

In floorball, the determined play positions are more or less passed in the history. Positions are changed and rotated all the time during the game. A defender can lift up the play and end up scoring in the opponents' slot. Therefore young players

3.团队战术

团队战术是指在比赛过程中采用的能够维持整个球队有条不紊的秩序和规范的球队作战体系，同时使球员清楚在自己所处的位置该运用什么样安全有效的打法。当五名球员同时在赛场上时，他们应该明白在不同的位置自己的任务是什么，有团队战术的指导，队员更容易意识到队友的下一步行动。

对教练而言，团队战术有助于发挥每一名队员的最佳优势。根据每个队员的能力——身体上的或思想上的——设置球员的位置，这是利用团队战术的最佳方式。

但是在旱地冰球中，固定位置的打法已经基本成为历史了。比赛过程中，球员的位置是在不停的改变和流转的，防卫队员可能会扭转战局，最终将球打进对方球门。因此年轻的队员必须掌

should be taught to play all different positions. Every player should also at least once try as a goalkeeper.

Some other characteristics in floorball today can be seen in the team play system of the top leagues.

A winning team bases its tactics on offensive play. There are practically two different ways to attack; organized attacks and transition (counter attacks).

Some teams rely on holding the possession of the ball by slow and strictly organized attacks but the trend in the top leagues is to base the offensive play on straight forward attacks with short distances and one time passes using all five players in a unified front. When the defensive team is standing still in the fore checking figure, they are easily outplayed by speed and quick ball moving. This demands a lot from the players, such as technical capacity to execute

握在不同位置的打法，每一名队员也应当至少尝试做一次守门员。

现在联盟中一些顶尖的球队往往会采用其他的团队战术。

获胜球队依赖于他的进攻战术。切实可行地有两种进攻打法：有组织的进攻和快攻（反攻）。

有些球队依赖控球并通过组织严密的慢攻打法，但是联盟中的顶尖球队倾向于组织短距离直接进攻的打法，五名球员在前场一次性传球联合进攻。当防守队员仍然保持前场的阵形时，对方可以通过速度和快速传球取胜。这对球员个人的能力要求很高，例如准确的一传到位技术能力以及对整场比赛的把握能力。

第二章　旱地冰球运动的基本技术战术
Chapter Two　The Basic Techniques and Tactics of Floorball

accurate one time passes and ability to read the game.

Another offensive tactic is transition. Transition from defense to offence demands a lot of skills and reaction speed, but can be a weapon that the opponent has no chance to beat, with no time to organize the defense. Counter attacks can only be beaten with quick return from offence to defense which also should be practiced.

另一种进攻战术是快攻。从防守方转变为进攻方需要很多技巧和反应速度，但同时也是会使对方在短时间内无法组织进攻进而毫无还击之力的绝佳武器。同样，击败快攻也只有通过从进攻方迅速转为防守方，当然这需要多加练习。

In the defensive play the most used for checking figures are 1-2-2 with a directing top player and man cover in the defensive zone, and the classical 2-1-2.

防守打法最常使用的是1-2-2阵，其中技术最好的球员作为引领，将防守区域全覆盖，另外也会采用经典的2-1-2阵形。

The aim of this material is not to give the optimal solution to the question which team tactic is the best. The objective is also not to give an answer to which system a team should use, but more or less it help the coach to come up with the optimal system for the team and to explain the factors affecting that decision.

Different offensive and defensive system are handled at a basic level. Also exercises to practice these systems are included. The main emphasis on these exercises is on the individual skills needed in the specific system and on developing those skills and the ability to make decisions in specific team tactical situations.

本教材的目的不是来回答哪一种团队战术最好，也不是为了解答球队应当使用怎样的战术体系，但或多或少能给教练提供一个理想的模式，并说明影响该决定的因素。

不同的进攻和防守战术体系都须从最初级水平开始，经多次训练。训练着重强调团队战术中所需的个人技术及特殊的团队战术中该个人技术的发展，以及决策能力的提升。

第三章　无处不在的旱地冰球运动
Chapter Three　Floorball Game is Everywhere

Section One: Street Floorball

第一节　街头旱地冰球

Street Floorball has been played in Finland for over 10 years. The Street Floorball Tour ends in the Highlight of the tour, the Street Floorball Final, getting more popular every year. There are six different series played: men, women, girls under 16, boys under 16, mixed teams and companies.

　　The Street Floorball tournaments are played in different parts of Finland and the regional tournaments are organized by regional clubs in cooperation with the Street Floorball partners, which guarantee that all the tournaments have the same look

　　街头旱地冰球在芬兰已有10多年的历史了。街头旱地冰球巡回赛每年以它最精彩的部分——日益受欢迎的街头旱地冰球决赛而告落幕。比赛有六个系列：男子组、女子组、16岁以下女子组、16岁以下男子组、男女混合组以及公司组。

　　芬兰街头旱地冰球锦标赛在芬兰不同地区举办，而地区锦标赛是由其旱地冰球俱乐部与街头旱地冰球合作伙伴共同举办的，确保所有锦标赛具有相同的观赏效果和气氛。国家旱地冰球联合

and feel. The National Federation is responsible for the match schedules for each event and the marketing partners. The final tournament, where the winners of each tournament challenge each other, is also organized by the National Federation.

会负责各赛事的赛程安排以及市场营销。锦标赛决赛由各地区冠军进行角逐，也由国家旱地冰球联合会举办。

Street floorball rules:

1) The game is played 3 versus 3, without goalkeepers.

2) The game time is 1×12 minutes.

3) The game is played within a rink and the recommendable field is 10m×20m, but can be changed depending on the conditions.

4) Small goals are used. The recommendable goal size is 60cm×40cm(width×height).

5) There is a goal area with a 150cm ray and with the form of a half circle.

街头旱地冰球规则：

1) 3对3，无守门员；

2) 比赛仅一节，12分钟；

3) 比赛使用有挡板场地，正规场地规格为10米×20米，但根据条件可以调整；

4) 使用小球门，正规球门尺寸为60厘米×40厘米(宽×高)；

5) 赛场设有一个半径为1.5米的半圆形区域，为禁区；

第三章　无处不在的旱地冰球运动
Chapter Three　Floorball Game is Everywhere

6) The players are not allowed to touch the goal area with any body part, but playing with stick inside the goal is allowed.

7) The forwards' goal area offenses lead to a free-hit and the defenders' goal area offenses lead to penalty shots.

8) Penalty shots are performed from the middle point straight towards an empty net.

9) The ball needs to cross the goal line completely.

10) After a successful goal the game is continued after a game opening by the opponent in their own side of the field after the referee whistles. The opening cannot go straight to the goal. The match starts with a face-off.

11) In case the ball disappears from the field, the hit-in is performed by the team, which did not play the game outside the field. The hit-in is performed approximately one meter from

6) 禁止球员身体任何部位接触禁区，不过允许禁区内使用球杆；

7) 进攻方禁区内犯规判罚任意球，防守方禁区内犯规判罚点球；

8) 点球从赛场中心起罚，直接打向空门；

9) 球必须整体越过球门线；

10) 裁判吹哨示意射门有效后，由失分一方在本方场地开球继续比赛。开球不能直接射门，比赛以争球开始；

11) 防止球被打出场外，边线球由场外未进行比赛的球队队员发入场内。从场地底线边角发球，发球点距离边界1米；

北欧时尚运动——旱地冰球
Nordic Fashion Sport FLOORBALL

the board and from the corners in the ends.

12)The free-hits and hit-ins can go straight to the goal.

12) 任意球和边线球可以直接射门。

Chapter Three Floorball Game is Everywhere

Section Two: Sand Floorball and Swamp Floorball

Swamp Floorball and Sand Floorball are also popular versions of the game, which are emerging in more and more countries.

1. Rules of sand floorball

1) Sand Floorball is played with almost the same rules as Street Floorball without the goalies with small 40 cm × 60 cm goals.

2) There are three players from each team on the field at the same time and the size of the rink is about 20m × 10m.

3) It is recommended to play with bare feet and it is also recommended to use protective goggles to avoid sand in the eyes.

4) In this relaxed version of the game there are no penalties but in case of an offence a

第二节 沙上旱地冰球和沼泽旱地冰球

沼泽旱地冰球和沙上旱地冰球也是比较流行的比赛形式，出现在越来越多的国家。

1.沙上旱地冰球规则

1) 沙上旱地冰球的比赛规则基本与街头旱地冰球的规则一致，无守门员，使用尺寸为40厘米×60厘米的小球门；

2) 每支球队分别有三名上场球员，球场的尺寸为20米×10米；

3) 建议光脚打比赛，为避免沙子进入眼睛，建议队员佩戴护目镜；

4) 这种比较放松的比赛形式中无判罚规定，但如出现犯规，与街头旱地冰球相

北欧时尚运动——旱地冰球
Nordic Fashion Sport FLOORBALL

penalty shot is given in the same way as in Street Floorball. The game time is 1×12 minutes.

同，对犯规判罚球。比赛共计一节，时间为12分钟。

第三章　无处不在的旱地冰球运动
Chapter Three　Floorball Game is Everywhere

2. Rules of swamp floorball

2.沼泽旱地冰球规则

Swamp Floorball is played on a swamp in the nature with a plastic ball without holes. The

沼泽旱地冰球的比赛在天然的沼泽上进行，使用无孔的塑料球。比赛场地尺寸

game field is 25m×15m and is marked with hay bales. The goals are 2m×4m and the ball is 12cm in diameter. Otherwise the rules do not differ much from normal Floorball played inside a rink. The swamp nevertheless requires additional physical strength and one can say that there are two opponents, the players in the opposite team and the swamp.

为25米×15米，边线用干草堆做标记，球门2米高,4米宽，球直径12厘米。除此以外，沼泽旱地冰球和正规旱地冰球的场内比赛规则并没有太大的区别。不过沼泽旱地冰球却需要额外的体力，可以说一名队员有两个对手，一个是对方球队的球员，另一个便是沼泽地。

In order to enter new markets, IFF has also started a development process, together with the SP (Swedish Testing & Research Institute National) to make an outdoor ball on hardcourt fields (in countries, where there is a limited access to indoor halls).

Section Three: Youth Floorball

1.Floorball for children and youth

Floorball is mainly spread by introducing the sport to children and youth in new countries. The small children can play with modified rules, on small fields with smaller goals and a goalkeeper is not necessarily needed. The playing time can be led by an elected game leader.

It is also important to stress important values of sports when working with young players or establishing the young activities. It is also essential to

为了进入新的市场，IFF与瑞典检测机构——SP进行合作，启动了一项发展程序，发展室外旱地冰球，使旱地冰球能够在(室内场馆有限的国家)室外硬场地上进行。

第三节 青少年旱地冰球

1.儿童和青少年的旱地冰球

在一些还未开展旱地冰球运动的国家普及该项目，主要是把它介绍给儿童和青少年。小孩子在打旱地冰球时可以适当调整规则，选用小场地，不一定非设守门员。比赛时间可以由选出的运动负责人掌握。

与年轻运动员合作或建立这一年轻的项目时，要着重强调运动的重要价值。另外，向当地相关管理机构介

第三章　无处不在的旱地冰球运动
Chapter Three　Floorball Game is Everywhere

stress the positive attitudes and values within Floorball when presenting projects to the local authorities. The children's and youth activities should focus on: establishing a safe learning environment, on joy and happiness, fair play and on the importance of everyone participating in the game.

2.The guidelines and aims of floorball for youth

1)To create a life-long interest for sports and Floorball.

2)To give everyone the possibility to participate.

3)Can be practiced with joy and played as starting points.

4)To give equal opportunities for girls and boys.

5)Can be played everywhere with modifiable rules, 3 vs. 3 etc.

6)To teach the youth that

绍这一运动项目时，一定要强调旱地冰球中所包含的积极的态度和价值所在。儿童和青少年活动的关键是：创造一个安全的学习环境，运动的趣味性、公平性，每个人的参与度。

2.青少年旱地冰球的指导方针和目标

1) 旨在培养青少年对运动和旱地冰球运动的终生兴趣；

2) 促使每个人都能参与到这个运动项目中；

3) 旱地冰球要充满趣味性，让它成为运动的起点；

4) 男孩和女孩机会均等；

5) 通过调整规则，旱地冰球随处可玩，如3打3等；

6) 旱地冰球教导青少

companionship and security can be reached with good team spirit and attitude as well as positive approach within and outside the rink.

7)To encourage the youth to engage in versatile leisure hobbies and school work.

3.Youth start up kit and youth programs

IFF has built a Floorball Youth Start Up Kit for teaching Floorball to youngsters, in which the important values in youth sports are stressed. This material has been produced in English, French, German, Italian, Spanish, Portuguese, Russian, Chinese Mandarine and Korean.

The Youth Start Up Kit has been the major development document for youth and the school sports, since it gives a clear view on how to start playing, what you need and the rules of the game in a nutshell. The material has been amended

年，不管是在赛场上还是在场下，只要有良好的团队精神、态度和正确的方式，就能保证协作和安全；

7) 鼓励青少年要热衷于多样的课余爱好和学业。

3.青少年入门手册及青少年项目规划

为了给青少年进行旱地冰球培训，IFF专门编写了旱地冰球青少年入门手册，着重强调青少年运动的重要价值。该手册已被翻译成英语、法语、德语、意大利语、西班牙语、葡萄牙语、俄语、汉语及韩语。

青少年入门手册现已成为青少年以及校内运动发展的主要支撑材料，该入门手册简明扼要的说明了如何开展旱地冰球这项运动、运动所需及简明比赛规则。另外，根据使用者的反馈信

第三章　无处不在的旱地冰球运动
Chapter Three　Floorball Game is Everywhere

based on the feedback given from users.

Get to know the schooling system beforehand, so that you know who to approach and how. You have to get the teachers' attention in order to gain entry to the school curriculum. In most countries the sports should first be approved by the teachers, before it is allowed to be taught in schools.

息，这些材料一直在进行相应的修订。

如果要向学校推荐旱地冰球运动，要事先理清楚该校行政系统，搞清楚和谁联系，如何联系。旱地冰球运动一定要吸引老师的注意力，才有获准列入该校课程的机会。在大多数国家，一项运动首先要得到教师认可，然后才能进行教学活动。

When you have access to the schools, try to get as many pupils/students to get involved in a club. Perhaps they might even

当旱地冰球运动获准进入学校后，要尽可能多的让学生参与到俱乐部中。甚至

start their own club with a little assistance.

Floorball is one of the most popular sports in the schools in which the sport has been introduced. The popularity of Floorball in both the pupils and teachers eyes derives from the fact that Floorball is one of the few team sports in which everyone can participate. It can be fun even though one does not yet master the sport. It is a sport which can be played in mixed teams and it is also quite inexpensive for the schools to buy Floorball equipment packages for the pupils.

As a specific youth programme IFF has also started cooperation with ISF, organizing the World School Championships, which has already increased the number of countries where Floorball is being played in schools.

如果给予一些帮助，他们可以成立自己的俱乐部。

旱地冰球是被引进学校最受欢迎的运动项目之一。在老师和学生眼中，旱地冰球是为数不多的团队运动项目之一，任何人都能够参与其中，这是旱地冰球如此受欢迎的原因所在。即便你还没能很好地掌握这项运动，同样可以从中获得很多乐趣。旱地冰球也可以组成男女混合的球队，而且对学校而言，为学生购买运动装备开销并不太大。

作为一项专门的青少年项目规划，IFF已经与国际垒球联合会合作，共同举办世界旱地冰球学校冠军赛。这使得开展校内旱地冰球运动的国家数量猛增。

第三章　无处不在的旱地冰球运动
Chapter Three　Floorball Game is Everywhere

4. Spreading floorball amongst youth

Source: GBFUA (Great Britain Floorball & Unihockey Association).

The youth development committee was set up to promote Floorball in GB in May 2007.

5. Partnership and support

Several meetings with various coordinators were arranged and from this we were invited into schools and the sports centre to

4.普及青少年旱地冰球

资料来源：英国旱地冰球及冰球协会。

青少年发展委员会于2007年5月成立，旨在英国推广旱地冰球运动。

5.合作伙伴和赞助

与不同的企业协调人参加了几次会议后，我们受邀到一些学校和运动中心去介

promote Floorball. The GBFUA has been part of a government initiative that has provided schools with extra money to provide extra activities for young people.

With regard to local government we have a young player employed as a Floorball coach by county council. In education we coach in schools and also we have Floorball on school curriculum as part of examinations.

绍推广旱地冰球运动。英国旱地冰球及冰球协会拥有政府支持，政府可以给学校提供资金，为青少年开展额外的活动项目。

我们为郡政府聘任一位年轻的运动员担任旱地冰球教练。在教育方面，我们在学校进行培训，并将旱地冰球纳入学校考试课程体系。

6. Youth involvement and training

6.青少年的参与及训练

There is a level 1 coaching course in Floorball, referee course and first aid/health and safety at work course all of which are a requirement for insurance which our coaches have. The level 1 course is offered to 15 years old and up to adults only. In the referee junior course there

旱地冰球有一级教练课程、裁判课程及急救与安全培训课程，所有课程都是教练所必须的，以确保训练的安全。一级教练课程只对15岁及以上的成年人开设，初级裁判员培训也允许9岁大

第三章　无处不在的旱地冰球运动
Chapter Three　Floorball Game is Everywhere

are 9 years old attending. At the league matches it is the young players that referee and scribe.

7. Key steps to success

The youth project has been so successful due to the following reasons:

1) Working committee. All of us have a task to do and we call regular meetings and feedback.

2) Working with UK sport trust, active in Gloucester and sport England. Taking advice and guidance and also supporting these organizations by being active part of sports programs.

3) Professionalism. When we go to schools or other youth organization we have a kit comprising of track suit and shirt with GB Youth Floorball printed on back.

4) We provide lesson plans and information before we go to event that way the staff have an

的青少年参加。俱乐部联赛通常由青少年运动员担任裁判和记录员。

7. 成功的关键步骤

青少年项目之所以如此成功取决于如下原因：

1) 工作委员会。所有的工作人员各司其职，召开常规会议，及时反馈；

2) 与在格罗斯特和英国运动界表现十分活跃的英国运动信托合作。虚心接受建议和指导，并且通过积极参与部分运动项目来支持这些组织的运行；

3) 专业品质。我们去学校或者其他青少年组织走访时一定会着专门装备，包括场地运动服和后背印有英国旱地冰球字样的衬衫；

4) 我们在举办赛事之前会给工作人员提供课程安排

idea as to what to expect and can ensure that we are coaching to students ability.

5)We are very fortunate in that we have on committee a learning disability teacher who has written coaching guidelines for young people with specific learning and difficulties. This is also an excellent resource for coaches.

和介绍各类信息，这样他们就能清楚我们会做什么，从而确信我们能够帮助学生提高能力和水平；

5) 十分幸运的是，委员会有一名负责学习障碍的老师专门为有学习障碍的青年撰写的教练手册，这本手册也是教练很好的素材；

6) Only qualified coaches attend awareness, we do take young players to assist awareness sessions and training in schools.

6) 有资格的教练才能进行运动员的意识训练，当然我们的确会让一些年轻的球员协助进行意识培训和在学校的训练工作；

Chapter Three　Floorball Game is Everywhere

7) We find and support organizations to apply for government funding. Youth Floorball groups so far have received approximately £30,000 for Floorball equipment and to attend tournaments.

8) Youth league matches are free. The adult league each team has to pay £100 to play at each match plus £50 to register the team. This is expensive and thus does not encourage new teams.

9) The biggest success of our project is our youth coaches and referees. It is these young people who do all training in schools, apply for grants and actively promote Floorball.

8. School road show

An example from Finland

Source: FFF.

The School Road Show is a fun activity day, through which Floorball clubs in Finland can promote Floorball and their own

7) 我们积极寻找并鼓励各机构申请政府基金。青少年旱地冰球目前已经收到大约3万英镑的资金，用于购买装备和参加锦标赛；

8) 青少年联赛免费参与，成年组联赛每支球队需要缴纳100英镑的参赛金，并且需要额外支付50英镑注册费。这些开销都不便宜也不利于鼓励新球队；

9) 这个项目最大的成功之处在于我们的青年教练和裁判员。正是这些年轻人在学校进行培训、申请拨款并且积极推广旱地冰球。

8.学校路演

来自芬兰的案例

资料来源：芬兰旱地冰球联合会。

学校路演是一个趣味十足的活动日，这天芬兰的旱地冰球俱乐部可以借此机会宣传自己的俱乐部、帮助推

clubs. The Finnish Floorball Federation provides the clubs with a readymade package, including a rink, accuracy shooting fabric, sticks, vests and goggles for eye protection.

 The School Road Show is organized by the Federation in cooperation with its partners. For the schools the School Road Show provides an opportunity to organize an entertaining sports day with Floorball. All the participating children receive a Road Show pass and a gift from the partners.

 The School Road Show is organized in cooperation with local Floorball clubs. The clubs can use the material package free of charge and can promote their own Floorball clubs through the Road Show. The School Road Show can also be organized as a part of a multisport event in cooperation with the National Sports Committees regional offices or as a single School event based on applications from schools.

广旱地冰球。芬兰旱地冰球联合会给这些俱乐部提供现成的装备，包括场地、精准球门、球杆若干、队服背心及护目镜。

 学校路演是芬兰旱地冰球联合会与其合作伙伴共同举办的一个活动，旨在为学校提供机会，利用旱地冰球开展趣味盎然的运动日。参加这项活动的青少年都有机会获得路演通行证和旱地冰球联合会的合作伙伴提供的礼品一份。

 地方旱地冰球俱乐部协助组织学校路演，俱乐部可以免费使用装备，利用路演的机会宣传自己。学校路演也可以作为国家运动委员会的地区机构合作举办的多项运动赛事的一部分，或者根据学校的申请作为一项独立的学校赛事。

第三章　无处不在的旱地冰球运动
Chapter Three　Floorball Game is Everywhere

9.Floorball in universities

9.大学里的旱地冰球

The development of floorball started in universities as it was the students who brought and spread the sport to Europe. Usually universities are quite international and it is easy to connect people around the world. Therefore one primary target group could be the university alumnus.

Floorball has for example spread through universities in China and Portugal.

　　旱地冰球的发展源于大学，正是学生们将这项运动引进欧洲并在欧洲推广。通常大学相当国际化，较容易与其他国家的人取得联系，因此推广的主要目标群之一就是大学校友。

　　旱地冰球在中国和葡萄牙就是通过这种方式传播的。

10. Floorball development through universities

In China the first floorball coaching seminar for the PE teachers in Beijing districts was organized in Jiu Hua Resort in December 2007 in order to introduce the sport to schools. The seminar was conducted by IFF and organized by Beijing Education and Science Research Institution in cooperation with a sport company. Approximately 100 teachers taking part in the two-day seminar, which included lectures about the rules and basic techniques as well as practical training sessions.

Floorball was introduced to Shanghai in 2008 by a PE teacher in Shanghai International Studies University. With the support of Shanghai based foreign club members, they held the first floorball training session for PE teachers in Shanghai universities, in which 38 teachers from over 20 universities were trained. After that, students

10. 旱地冰球在大学的发展

北京：中国首个旱地冰球教练研讨会于2007年11月在九华山庄召开，专为北京地区体育老师而设，旨在将这项运动介绍给学校。此次研讨会由国际旱地冰球联合会指导，由北京教育科学研究机构与某个体育用品有限公司合作。约有100名老师参加了本次为期两天的研讨会，内容涵盖旱地冰球基本规则、基本技能以及训练等。

上海：上海旱地冰球运动的发展是由上海外国语大学一位体育老师引进。在上海的外籍球员俱乐部的帮助下，2008年底举办了第一期培训，参加的38位大学体育老师来自20所高校。培训结束后，上海共有5所大学的学生们率先体验到旱地冰球

第三章　无处不在的旱地冰球运动
Chapter Three　Floorball Game is Everywhere

from 5 universities experienced the interesting game for the first time.

After floorball was taken into curriculum for two years, the first Shanghai Floorball Tournament was held in 2009 and over 100 students participated. The primary promotion attracted the attention of many universities and colleges, and made enough preparation for the future development. After the successful second Shanghai Floorball Tournament for College Students in 2010, Mr. John Liljelund, Secretary General of International Floorball Federation(IFF) was invited by Shanghai University Sports Federation to train the coaches and referees in Shanghai. 45 teachers from 24 universities and high schools received the training. Mr. Liljeland highly praised the enthusiasm of the teachers, and expressed his high expectations on the development of future floorball in China. He

的趣味和乐趣。

经过两年的教学，2009年举办首次上海旱地冰球邀请赛，100多名学生参赛，前期的推广吸引了很多高校目光也为后期的发展成功蓄势。2010年成功举办第二届上海大学生邀请赛后，上海大学生体育协会发函，邀请到IFF（国际旱地冰球联合会）秘书长约翰·雷杰伦先生到上海培训旱地冰球教练和裁判员（来自24所大学和中学的45位教师参加了培训），雷杰伦先生高度评价

老师的热情并对中国旱地冰球运动发展寄予厚望，也表

said he would spare no effort to provide more support to the development of floorball in China.

示会对旱地冰球在中国的发展给于更多的支持。

Later on, floorball was successfully accepted as a part of Shanghai Sunshine Sports League. Hence she received the acknowledgement and support from Shanghai Education Commission. In order to improve

接着我们又将旱地冰球成功申请加入了上海市阳光体育大联赛，从而得到了上海市教委的承认和大力支持。为了实现高质量的比赛，2011年上半年专业的新

第三章　无处不在的旱地冰球运动
Chapter Three　Floorball Game is Everywhere

the quality of the games, in 2011, professional referees from Singapore were invited to give the referees in Shanghi more profound and detailed training. Thus, a relatively professional referees team in Shanghai came into being, and their professional qualities have been improved in the following matches.

The year 2011 was of great significance for the development of floorball because apart from the previous achievements, two other large-scale tournaments were held in November. One, organized by Chen xin, was the friendship match between the teams of companies clubs and of universities, the other was organized as a part of the annual Shanghai Sunshine Sports League. The former succeeded in linking Chinese university students and some European players, who introduced the floorball to China, providing the students an opportunity to appreciate the European

加坡裁判获邀到上海为教师进行了更加细致深入的裁判培训。至此上海市拥有了一支较为规范的裁判队伍，他们也在后来的比赛中更加专业。

2011年是旱地冰球发展的大年，除了上述的成果外，11月又举办了两次有规模的比赛。一次是陈新组织的外籍俱乐部、高校友谊赛，另一次则是一年一度的上海市阳光体育大联赛。前者成功地把大学生同这项运动的引进者——欧洲人联系在一起，让大学生有幸一览外国人的精湛水平的同时也助推旱地冰球得到更多外国人的支持；后者总赛程达到两天半，是旱地冰球在上海的第一届官方比赛，意义相当深远。

players' perfect skills. The game also made the European players more willing to offer their support for floorball in China. The latter, with a schedule of two and a half days, was the first official game in Shanghai and was far reaching.

Then December that year witnessed the first floorball promotion training in the middle western area of China, organized by PE teachers in China University of Geosciences (Wuhan). Up to now, there have already ten universities and three middle schools in Shanghai have set floorball in P.E. curriculum and formed their teams. In 2012, floorball has been introduced to the following provinces & cities:

另外，2011年12月在中国地质大学（武汉校区）体育部教师的组织下，第一次在中国中西部地区进行旱地冰的培训。截至目前为止，上海市已经有10所大学和3所中学开设旱地冰球课程并建立运动队。2012年已在湖北、四川、黑龙江、吉林、福建、珠海等有意向发展的的几个省市和地区推广，这

第三章 无处不在的旱地冰球运动
Chapter Three Floorball Game is Everywhere

Hubei, Sichuan, Heilongjiang, Jilin, Fujian and Zhuhai, where universities and schools have expressed their interest to promote the sport. It is promising that in 2013 and the coming years more and more people will be attracted by floorball's charm and it will, by leaps and bounds, give rise to a craze for this sport in every corner of the country.

些省市和地区高校及中学已有发展旱地冰球的意向。 相信在2013年及以后，旱地冰球一定会以它的魅力令更多人为之折服，并以迅捷之势传至全国各地。

Section Four: Floorball in Companies

Floorball is one of the most popular sports played by different companies in the big Floorball countries. There are a lot of different company leagues playing the game, for example the police, lawyers, sport journalists and teachers as well as rock musicians, they can have their own leagues and tournaments.

　　The company leagues can be organized either by the National Floorball Federation, Floorball Arenas or Company Unions. Usually the National Floorball Federation supports these leagues by providing know-how and equipment. The basic idea is that the Company Union provides the teams (for example six lawyer firms) who want to challenge each other. Each team (company) pays a participation fee to the Floorball Arena (or other

第四节　公司里的旱地冰球

　　在旱地冰球比较风靡的国家，它是最受社团组织欢迎的运动项目。打旱地冰球的公司社团类型很多，如警察、律师、体育记者、教师甚至还有摇滚音乐人，他们拥有自己的社团并组织比赛。

　　组建公司社团的可以是国家旱地冰球联合会、旱地冰球竞技组织或者由企业联盟组织。通常国家旱地冰球联合会都会给这些社团提供技术指导和装备支持。基本理念是公司社团能够给这些团队（譬如六个律师事务所）一个挑战彼此的机会。每个团队都需要向旱地冰球竞技组织（或者其他组织机构）缴纳参赛费，以得到场

第三章　无处不在的旱地冰球运动
Chapter Three　Floorball Game is Everywhere

organizing body) that provides the team the field, sticks, vests, a referee and the statistics and points tables. To get both genders to participate equally, some leagues have rules that there must be at least one woman (one out of five field players) on the field all the time.

It is always better to approach people in already existing groups such as companies. As they might offer you the facilities and funding, you can in return offer them introductory lessons or organize events or tournaments.

The Floorball Points Master and Street Floorball are also very popular versions of the game, which are played in different companies.

地、球队背心、裁判、数据和得分表等基本设备。为确保男女均等的参赛资格，有些社团规定，场上必须保证至少一名女性球员（五名上场球员之一）。

最好是能够联系到社团里（如公司）的人，因为他们可能为你提供装备和资金支持，作为回报，你则可以为他们提供旱地冰球入门课程或者组织赛事。

旱地冰球得分赛制和街头旱地冰球也是比赛中很受欢迎的形式，很多公司都组织这样的比赛。

中国旱地冰球信息网 www.floorballinfo.com
国际旱地冰球联合会 www.floorball.org

第四章　旱地冰球运动的综合技术
Chapter Four　The Basic Technique of Floorball

Terms and figures used　术语及图例

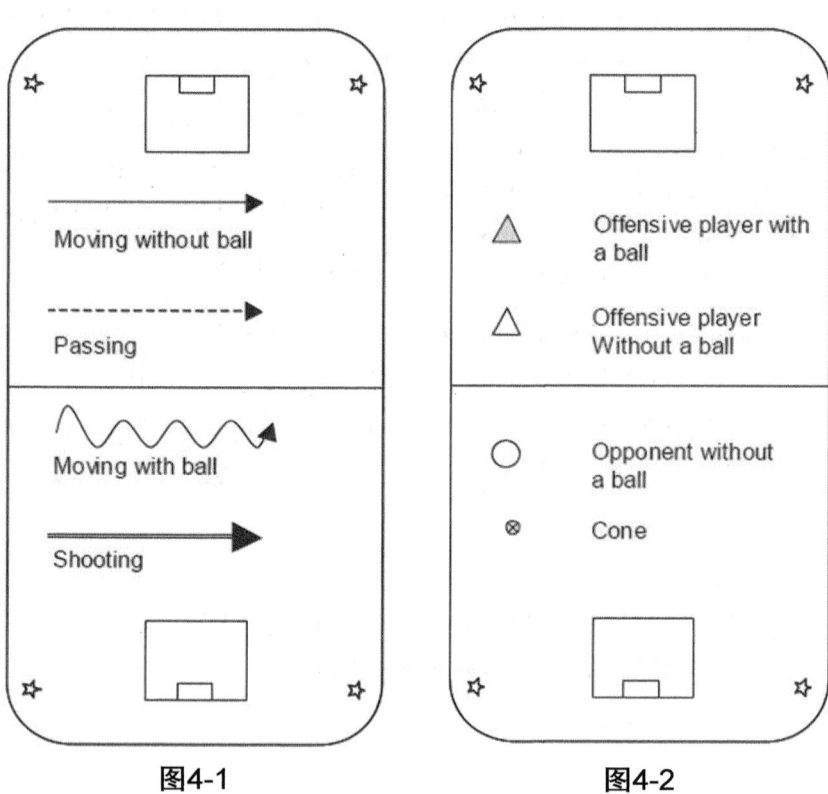

图4-1　　　　　　　　图4-2

第四章 旱地冰球运动的综合技术
Chapter Four The Basic Technique of Floorball

Section One: The Training of Basic Technique

The right posture and grip are both introduced in Section one of Chapter two. So this section will focus on the exercises and practice of the basic technique in detail.

第一节 综合技术的练习

第二章第一节已介绍过正确的站位和握杆姿势，因此本小节将对综合技术的训练和操作进行详细介绍。

1.Passing and receiving

Level 1

The most important thing to emphasize for the beginners is that each pass should be accurate

1.传、接球

第一阶段

初学者应着重掌握的是每个传球都必须精准，且传球力度适中，传球力度视场

and the hardness should be suited to the situation.

Technically the important things in passing and receiving are the posture and the grip (Which had been introduced in Section one of Chapter two).

The posture and grip change slightly according to different techniques but cushion and softness matter a lot when handling the ball. The distance between players is an important factor while defining the speed and hardness of the pass. All other objects, such as the opponent, sticks and boards should also be noticed while determining the right passing technique.

上情况而定。

从技术层面上讲，传接球比较重要的两点是站位和握杆姿势（见第二章第一节）。

站位和握杆姿势可以根据不同的技巧进行微调，但有一点很重要，那就是在控球的时候一定要注意缓冲、用力要轻柔。球员之间的距离是传接球时确定速度和力道的一个重要因素，同时，对手、球杆和挡板等都是使用恰当传球技术的影响因子。

中国旱地冰球信息网 www.floorballinfo.com
国际旱地冰球联合会 www.floorball.org

第四章 旱地冰球运动的综合技术
Chapter Four The Basic Technique of Floorball

Drill 1

Objective:

To practice passing and receiving.

Organization:

Players divided in pairs passing to each other in varied distances.

Execution:

1) Using all passing techniques in random order.

2) Receiving the pass using only stick or body, or both.

常规训练1

训练目的：

训练传接球。

训练安排：

运动员分两组，按不同距离传球。

训练步骤：

1) 自由运用所有的传球技术；

2) 仅用球杆或身体接球，或两者兼用。

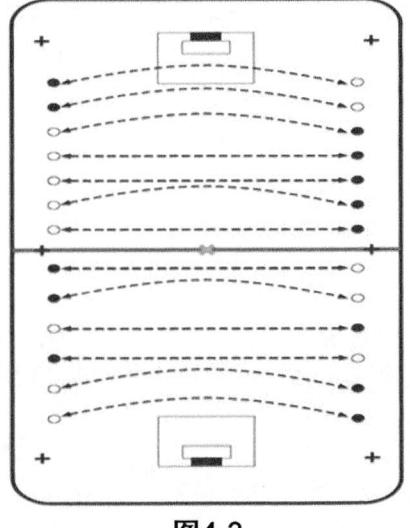

图4-3

Modifications:

Can also be executed individually using the boards, in aerial passes using a wall.

说明：

个人练习时可以使用挡板，接高球时使用墙壁。

北欧时尚运动——旱地冰球
Nordic Fashion Sport FLOORBALL

Key points:

1)Head up.

2)Game like position; on toes, knees slightly bent.

3)Correct grip according to the passing technique.

4)Player should always move towards the ball while receiving a pass.

5)The stick should be between the body and the ball while receiving an aerial pass (if the stick is on the side of the body, it demands more ball handling skills to capture the ball, therefore it is easier to lose the possession of the ball).

训练要点：

1) 保持抬头；

2) 模拟赛场站位，脚趾发力，双膝微弯曲；

3) 根据传球技术修正握杆姿势；

4) 球员在接球时注意向来球方向移动（迎球）；

5) 接高球时球杆在身体和球之间（如果球杆在体侧，则要求更高超的技术才能接到并控好球，因此更容易失球）。

第四章 旱地冰球运动的综合技术
Chapter Four The Basic Technique of Floorball

Drill 2

Objective:

1) To practice passing and receiving aerial passes.

2) Good exercise for eye-stick coordination.

Organization:

Players are divided in pairs with one ball.

Execution:

1) Pairs are passing the ball to each other in air.

2) Emphasis on the taking control of the ball as quickly as possible when receiving an aerial pass.

Modifications:

Either one bounce on the floor allowed or no bounces.

Key points:

1) Right distance (depending on the bounces).

2) Eyes on the ball.

常规训练2

训练目的：

1) 练习传接高空球；

2) 眼杆协调练习。

训练安排：

两人一球分组训练。

训练步骤：

1) 两人进行传高球训练；

2) 训练重点在于接高空球后尽快控好球。

说明：

球触地弹起不超过一次。

训练要点：

1) 调整距离（取决于球触地后是否反弹）；

2) 眼睛盯球；

3)Remaining relaxed in both hands and knees will help the player to control the aerial pass quicker.

3)保持双手和膝盖放松，有助于球员接到高球后迅速控球。

中国旱地冰球信息网 www.floorballinfo.com
国际旱地冰球联合会 www.floorball.org

第四章 旱地冰球运动的综合技术
Chapter Four The Basic Technique of Floorball

Drill 3

Objective:

To practice passing and receiving (while moving).

Organization:

Players are divided in pairs with one ball.

Execution:

Dribbling from the forehand to backhand side after receiving a pass, taking few steps forward, then passing and taking a few steps back after making the pass.

Modifications:

Also a rotation can be added after receiving a pass before passing back.

Key points:

Players should stay in constant movement using quick hands.

常规训练3

训练目的：

跑动过程中的传接球。

训练安排：

两人一球分组训练。

训练步骤：

接球后从正手运球至反手侧，向前数步后传球，再后退数步。

说明：

接球后，回传球时也可加入身体的转动练习。

训练要点：

队员时刻处于移动状态，手要快。

北欧时尚运动——旱地冰球
Nordic Fashion Sport FLOORBALL

Drill 4

Objective:

1) To practice passing and receiving (while moving).

2) To practice readiness to pass and to receive a pass.

3) To practice ball handling skills.

Execution:

1) Groups of three.

2) Two players standing with 10-15 meters distance between them.

3) Third player in the middle with a ball.

Execution:

1) The player in the middle runs back and forth with the ball passing a one-timer to the other two at each turn.

常规训练4

训练目的：

1) 跑动过程中练习传接球；

2) 练习随时传接球；

3) 练习控球技术。

训练安排：

1) 三人一组；

2) 其中两名队员间隔10－15米；

3) 第三名队员持球站在中间。

训练步骤：

1) 中间队员持球来回跑动，每一轮分别传球至另两名队员其中一名；

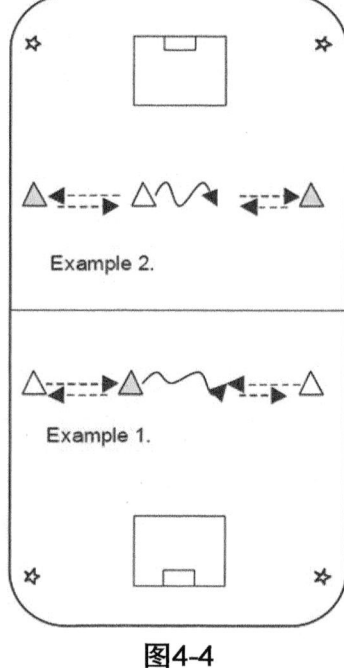

图4-4

第四章　旱地冰球运动的综合技术
Chapter Four　The Basic Technique of Floorball

2)5-60 second shifts.

Modifications:

Drill can also be executed so that the two players have one ball each and the third player runs without a ball passing a one-timer at each turn.

The emphasis is on practicing the readiness to pass and receive.

Key points:

1) Head up.

2) Soft hands.

3) Game like position with all players.

4) Timing and readiness to pass and receive.

5) Blade on the floor.

Level 2

When the players have learnt the passing techniques or one technique at a time if wished to proceed that way, the coach can add more difficult exercises to the practice. The game likeness

2) 50到60秒一轮换。

说明：

也可以两名队员每人持一球，第三名队员不持球来回跑动，每次跑动时接两名队员的一击传球；

练习重点在于随时传接球。

训练要点：

1) 保持抬头；

2) 手的力度柔和；

3) 所有队员模拟比赛位；

4) 传接球及时反应；

5) 击球板放在地板上。

第二阶段

如果队员已经掌握了传球技术，或者每次训练都掌握了一项技能且达到了预期目的，教练可以在训练中增加一些带有难度的内容。训练时一定要营造赛场的感

should be brought into exercises, and the reason why passing and receiving is important skills to manage, and in which types of situations these skills are crucial.

Moving the ball in the game happens at speed and therefore should be trained in more complicated exercises where situations follow each other. For younger players it is essential to know that each ball should be passed so that the receiver is capable of gaining the possession of the ball instantly. Next thing to emphasize is passing while moving and timing.

The coach should always encourage the players to:

1) Pass in motion.

2) Always continue motion after a pass.

3) Receive a pass in motion by moving towards the pass or sideways – do not wait for the ball to come to you.

4) As a ball carrier to keep head up to locate other players.

觉，同时说明掌握传接球技术的重要性以及在何种情况下运用这些技术。

在比赛中球的转移是瞬间完成的，相应的训练也要在不断变化的复杂情况下进行。年轻队员务必清楚每个球都要及时传出，确保接球队员能够直接控制好球。还要着重练习跑动中和计时中的传球。

教练应当经常教导队员：

1) 在移动时传球；

2) 传球后继续跑位；

3) 接球时要向球传来的方向或者边路跑动（迎球）——不要站着等球向你传来；

4) 持球队员应该始终抬头关注确定其他队员的位置；

第四章 旱地冰球运动的综合技术
Chapter Four The Basic Technique of Floorball

5) As a non-ball carrier to create passing lanes by moving.

6) Readiness to pass and receive.

7) As a non-ball carrier to show the ball-carrier where to pass, by pointing out with a stick or by using other signals.

8) Shoot straight from a pass if there is a possibility.

5) 无球队员应该通过跑位给持球队员创造传球路线；

6) 时刻准备好接球、传球；

7) 无球队员可以运用球杆或用其他方式给持球队员指明传球位置；

8) 如果有机会，接到球后立即射门。

中国旱地冰球信息网 www.floorballinfo.com
国际旱地冰球联合会 www.floorball.org

Drill 5

Objective:

To practice passing and receiving while moving.

Organization:

1) Players are divided in groups of 5-7 players.

2) These units are divided in half, the other half standing on a line opposite the others with the ball.

3) 5-8 meters distance (can be varied).

4) One ball each group.

Execution:

1) The player with the ball (nr 1) passes to the player across (nr 2) and continues moving towards the pass.

常规训练5

训练目的：

跑动过程中的传、接球练习。

训练安排：

1) 队员5－7人分成一组；

2) 每组再分成两小队(A&B)，A小队队员站成一排，与持球的B小队队员相对；

3) 两小队距离5-8米（可变）；

4) 每组一球。

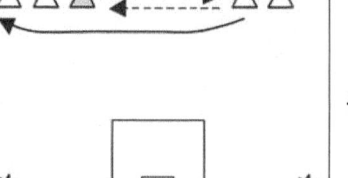

图4-5

训练步骤：

1) 持球队员（第一名队员）传球给对面队员（第二名队员），然后继续向对面跑动；

第四章　旱地冰球运动的综合技术
Chapter Four　The Basic Technique of Floorball

2)Player nr 2 passes the ball to player nr 3 and moves towards the pass and so on.

Modifications:

All different passes can be included; forehand passes, backhand passes, short aerial passes (more difficult to take control of).

Key Points:

1)Head up.

2)Continuous movement towards the pass.

3)All players are to move in the direction of their pass, moving to the end of the group.

4)Readiness to pass and receive a pass, blade on the floor,controlled passes not a race.

2) 第二名队员传球给第三名队员，第二名队员继续向传球方向跑动，以此类推。

说明：

练习所有不同传球方式，包括：正手传球，反手传球，短高球（较难控球）。

训练要点：

1) 保持抬头；

2) 持续向传球方向运动；

3) 所有队员朝传球方向跑动，最终跑至队伍末端；

4) 随时准备传接球，击球板放在地上，控制好传球，注意传接球并非赛跑。

中国旱地冰球信息网 www.floorballinfo.com
国际旱地冰球联合会 www.floorball.org

Drill 6

Objective:

1) To practice passing and receiving in movement.

2) To practice moving after a pass.

Organization:

1) Players are divided into groups of six in five positions (as in the picture 4-6), one ball each group.

2) All players stand in a circle in game like posture.

3) Two players in one position in the start, the first one with the ball.

4) Groups can add up to seven players.

Execution:

1) The player with the ball starts passing the ball in certain order.

2) After a pass the player has to follow the pass, that is to keep in constant motion.

常规训练6

训练目的:

1) 跑动过程中的传接球;

2) 练习持续跑位。

训练安排:

1) 队员6人一组,分别站在五个跑位上(如图4-6),每组一球;

2) 所有队员按照标准站位如图示站在圈内;

3) 开始时其中一个位置站两名队员,第一名队员持球;

4) 每组队员上限为7人。

训练步骤:

1) 第一名持球队员依特定顺序开始传球;

2) 传球后,队员仍需顺着传球的方向跑动,也就是持续跑位;

第四章 旱地冰球运动的综合技术
Chapter Four　The Basic Technique of Floorball

3) Players have to be sure about their ball handling skills to keep the head up and still maintain the control of the ball.

3) 队员必须有过硬的控球技巧，才能始终抬头并控制好球。

Modifications:

1) Can also be executed with passing in random order.

2) Calling can also be added so that the player with the ball has to shout the name of the players he/she is about to pass to.

3) Groups can add up to seven players.

Key points:

1) Keeping the head up.

2) Game like position.

3) Blade on the floor.

4) Be ready to receive a pass by turning early enough.

说明：

1) 也可以不按特定的顺序传球；

2) 练习中可以加入呼喊，队员通过喊出队友姓名来传球给他/她；

3) 每组队员上限为7人。

训练要点：

1) 保持抬头；

2) 比赛标准站位；

3) 击球板放在地上；

4) 尽量提前转身，准备好接球；

图4-6

5)Players are not allowed to pass to players next to them.

6)Emphasize communication/use of voice as an important tool on the court.

5) 队员不允许给自己旁边的球员传球;

6) 强调场上队员之间的交流、呼喊是重要方式。

第四章 旱地冰球运动的综合技术
Chapter Four The Basic Technique of Floorball

Drill 7

Objective:

1) To practice passing and receiving while moving with the ball.

2) To practice moving according to the ball carrier.

3) To practice choosing the right passing technique according to the situation.

4) Remind the players that there should always be three passing options.

Organization:

1) The players are divided into groups of five in a small area (5m × 5 m).

2) The area can be marked with cones.

3) One ball each group.

Execution:

1) Four of the players are passing the ball to each other keeping in constant motion.

常规训练7

训练目的：

1) 带球过程中的传接球练习；

2) 练习根据持球队员的位置进行跑位；

3) 按照具体情况选择正确传球技巧的练习；

4) 提醒球员传球方式有三种。

训练安排：

1) 小范围场地上(5米×5米)，球员5人一组；

2) 可用锥形标作为标记；

3) 每组一球。

训练步骤：

1) 4名队员分别传球给对方，并保持不断跑动；

2)One player in the middle is trying to steal the ball by cutting the passing lanes.

3)If the player in the middle touches the ball, he/she will switch places with the player who made the failed pass.

4)Players are supposed to stay in motion providing passing lanes to the player with the ball.

Modifications:

1)Players can also stand still when only one-time passes are allowed, but then the emphasis is more on moving the ball instead of players.

2)The player with the ball is not allowed to move.

3)Only aerial passes allowed.

Key points:

1)Keep in motion.

2)Readiness to pass and receive a pass.

2) 中间一名队员努力通过切断传球路线来断球；

3) 若中间那名球员触到球，那么他就和传运球失败的那名队员交换位置；

4) 队员需要不断跑动，来为持球队员创造传球路线。

说明：

1) 当只允许一次传球时，队员可保持不动，但此时重点不在球员盯防而在运球上；

2) 持球队员不能随意改变位置；

3) 只有传高球的时候可以移动位置。

训练要点：

1) 持续跑动；

2) 时刻做好传球和接球的准备；

第四章 旱地冰球运动的综合技术
Chapter Four   The Basic Technique of Floorball

3)Blade on the floor.

4)Players should stay inside the area to keep up the level of difficulty.

5)Player in the middle should be motivated to keep up and try to steal the ball even though it seems difficult.

3) 击球板放在地上；

4) 为保持训练难度球员必须在划定区域内跑动；

5) 尽管困难，中间球员仍应伺机断球。

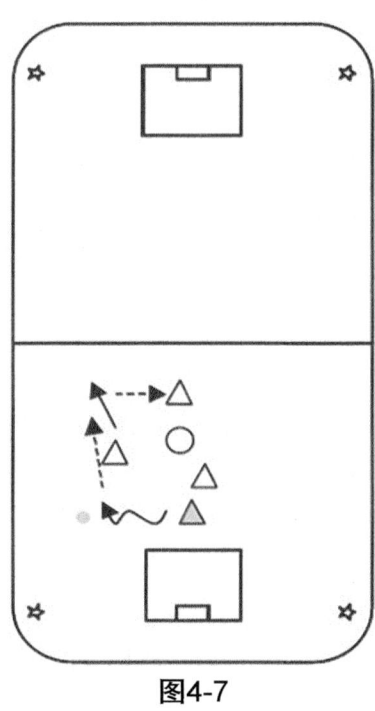

图4-7

Drill 8   常规训练8

Objective: 训练目的：

1) To practice passing and receiving while moving and gaining a scoring chance.

2) To learn how to avoid less effective scoring sectors and to advance straight to the net.

3) To shoot even from bad positions.

1）跑动过程中的传接球练习并创造射门机会；

2）学习如何避免无效射门区，直接靠近球门射门；

3）学习如何在不适合射门的站位上射门。

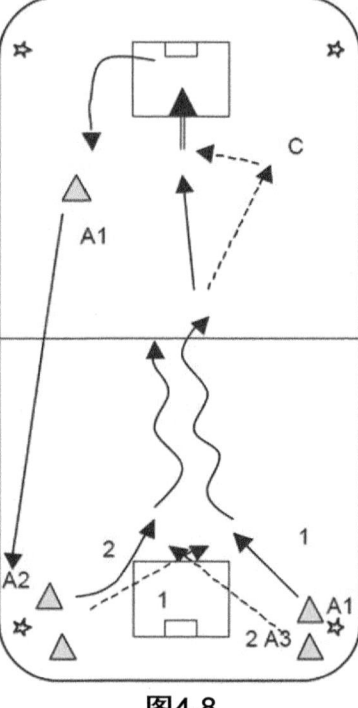

图4-8

Organization: 训练安排：

1) The coach should show where the less effective scoring sectors are (on the sides and in the corners) by placing cones on the spots.

2) Players line up in two corners with the balls.

3) Coach/trainee situated near the opposite goal ready

1）教练可以通过摆放锥形标，（在场边或四角）为队员指出射门机会较小的地方；

2）队员持球在两个角落排队训练；

3）教练／示范队员站在靠近对方球门的位置，准备

第四章 旱地冰球运动的综合技术
Chapter Four　The Basic Technique of Floorball

to receive a pass from the first player (after this his/her duty is done).

Execution:

1) A1 starts running without a ball slightly towards the centre.

2) A2 passes a ball to A1, who receives the pass in motion and continues towards the middle zone.

3) After crossing the middle line, A1 looks up and passes the ball to the coach/trainee, who passes a one-timer back and A1 shoots.

4) A1 moves on to the other side of the net to be ready to give a one-timer to the next player.

5) After the first pass, A2 starts by executing the same as A1, receiving a pass from A3 and then receiving the one-timer from A2.

6) After the execution the players will switch lines.

接第一名球员的传球（之后他／她的任务便完成了）。

训练步骤：

1) A1不持球，缓慢跑向中场；

2) A2传球给A1，A1在跑动过程中接球并继续向中场跑动；

3) 过中线后，A1抬头并传球给教练／示范队员，教练／示范队员回传一次给A1，A1射门；

4) A1跑动至球门另一侧，准备好一次传球给下一个球员；

5) 第一次传球后，A2重复A1所做动作，从A3处接球，然后从A2处得到回传；

6) 一轮训练之后两边队员互换场地。

Modifications:

1) The drill can be made more difficult by adding a defender in the play (nr 1 becomes a defender after giving a pass to nr 2).

2) Both the passer and the receiver have to be even more accurate with the passes and the movement is emphasized.

3) A variation with 2-0, the passer can also shoot.

4) This will teach the players to use their creativity in finishing attacks.

5) More options for the ball-carrier creating game like situations.

6) Movement emphasized

7) 2-1 with defender.

Key points:

1) Running slightly towards the first pass, not along the board.

2) Head up.

3) Quick shot straight from the pass, no matter in which position the player is or where the ball is passed to.

说明：

1) 通过增加一个防守队员，训练难度将会增加（1号传球给2号后，成为防守队员）；

2) 需要特别强调的是，传球队员和接球队员应当把握好传接球和跑位的精准度；

3) 当形势变成2比0时，传球队员可以射门；

4) 训练队员在进攻过程中发挥创造性；

5) 持球跑动的队员可以创造更多模拟赛事状况；

6) 跑位同样非常重要；

7) 有防守情况下运用2打1。

训练要点：

1) 慢慢跑向第一次传球处，勿沿挡板跑动；

2) 抬头；

3) 接到传球后直接射门，不管自己在什么位置，也不管球传向哪里。

第四章 旱地冰球运动的综合技术
Chapter Four The Basic Technique of Floorball

Drill 9	常规训练9

Objective:
1) To practtice passing and receiving in motion while gaining a scoring chance.

2) To learn how to avoid less effective scoring sectors and to advance straight to the net.

Organization:
1) Players form two lines in the opposite corners with balls.

2) One player is situated by the board at the middle line and one player in front of the net in respective ends of the rink.

Execution:
1) A1 starts by passing a hard and a long pass to B2.

2) B2 comes towards the pass, takes control of

训练目的：
1) 获得射门机会时跑动中传接球练习；

2) 学习如何避免无效射门区，进而直奔球网。

训练安排：
1) 队员持球在两对角站成2排；

2) 一名球员站在挡板中线处，另一名球员站在球场另一边的球门前。

训练步骤：
1) A1大力长传球给B2；

2) B2朝向传球方向接球并

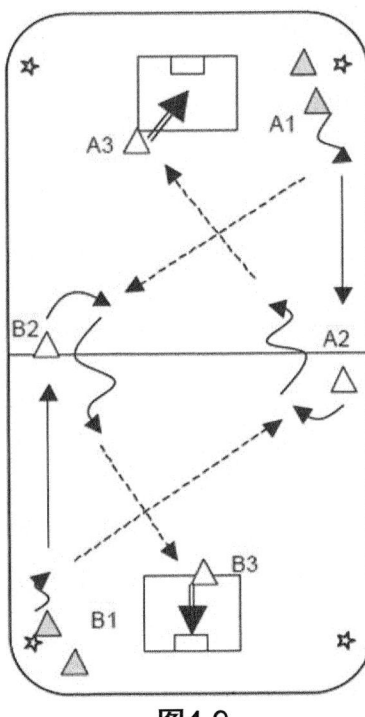

图4-9

the ball, makes a quick turn and passes the ball to the player on his/her own end of the rink, B3, who shoots.

3)On the other side, B1 passes the ball to A2, and A2 continues passing to A3, who shoots.

4)After the execution, A1 becomes A2, A2 becomes A3 and A3 becomes A1.

5)Same rotation in the other end (B1 becomes B2, B2 becomes B3 and B3 becomes B1).

6)After a while the drill should be executed as a mirror.

Modifications:

1)The drill could also be executed so that A1 passes to A2,and A2 to A3.

2)The situation can be seen as an opening which makes it more game like.

控球，迅速转身传球给自己半场在球门前的B3，B3射门；

3) 另一半场，B1传球给A2，A2继续传球给A3，A3射门；

4) 一轮训练后，A1变成A2，A2变成A3，A3变成A1；

5) 相应的，另一半场（B1变成B2,B2变成B3，B3变成B1）；

6) 一段时间后，两边形成一种镜像效果。

说明:

1) 训练也可变成：A1传球给A2，A2传球给A3；

2) 这种训练可被视作开场使训练更加类似于正式比赛。

第四章 旱地冰球运动的综合技术
Chapter Four The Basic Technique of Floorball

Key points:

1) A1 and B1 should start the drill simultaneously.

2) The players should be encouraged to receive the first pass with backhand (depending whether the player is left/right handed).

3) The passes should be accurate and hard.

4) A2 should go towards the first pass, all the way across the middle line.

5) A2 should keep in constant motion and head up to see where A3 is.

6) A1 should pass in motion and continue movement immediately after the pass towards the middle line for the next execution.

训练要点：

1) A1和B1应当同时间开始此训练项目；

2) 鼓励队员运用反手接第一次传球（视队员为左／右撇而定）；

3) 传球要精准大力；

4) A2要迎向第一次传球，并带球过中线；

5) A2应持续跑动，并抬头寻找A3；

6) A1应当在跑动中传球，当传球越过中线时立即继续向前跑动，准备下一轮训练。

中国旱地冰球信息网 www.floorballinfo.com
国际旱地冰球联合会 www.floorball.org

Level 3

Drill 10

Objective:

To practice passing and receiving while moving.

Organization:

1) Players divided into groups of five.

2) Three cones forming a triangle (5m×5m×5m).

3) Three players around the triangle and two players inside the triangle.

4) The players around the triangle has the possession of the ball.

Execution:

1) Players around the triangle are trying to pass the ball to each other using flat and aerial passes.

2) Players inside the triangle are trying to block the passing lanes.

第三阶段

常规训练10

训练目的：

跑动过程中的传接球练习。

训练安排：

1) 队员5人一组；

2) 三个锥形标围成三角形（5米×5米×5米）；

3) 三名队员围着三角形，两名队员在三角形内；

4) 三角形外围三名球员控球。

训练步骤：

1) 三角形外围队员应尽量传地滚球或高球给其他两名队员；

2) 三角形内队员应尽力阻断传球路线；

第四章　旱地冰球运动的综合技术
Chapter Four　The Basic Technique of Floorball

3)Whenever players outside succeed in crossing the both lines they score a point.

4)If a player inside succeeds in blocking the pass, the player will switch places with the player who missed the pass and the score will start over again.

5)Players around the triangle are allowed to move but there should always be two passing directions so they cannot stand behind the same side of the triangle.

Modifications:

1)Can also be executed by using a square with four players outside and three players inside.

2)Only two touches on the ball, one to receive the pass and the second to pass.

3) 三角形外围队员只要成功跨越两道防线，便可得分；

4) 若一名三角形内队员成功阻断传球路线，这一队员与接球失败的队员交换，计分清零；

5) 三角形外围队员可以跑动，但为确保有两个传球方向，因此他们不能站在三角形同一边上。

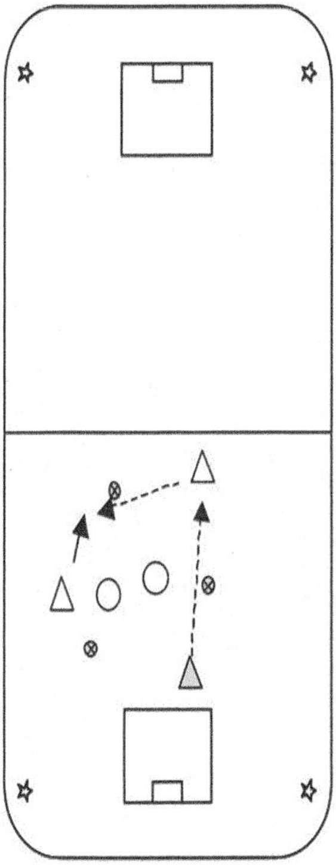

图4-10

说明：

1) 训练模式可变更为：用四个锥形标识围成正方形，4队员在外，3队员在内；

2) 只可触球两次；一次接球，另一次传球；

北欧时尚运动——旱地冰球

Nordic Fashion Sport FLOORBALL

Key Points:	训练要点:

1)It should be pointed out that there should always be two passing directions.

2)Head up.

3)The players outside the triangle are not allowed to cross the lines.

1) 需要说明的是，始终有两个传球方向；

2) 抬头；

3) 三角形外围队员不能跨过线。

中国旱地冰球信息网 www.floorballinfo.com

国际旱地冰球联合会 www.floorball.org

第四章 旱地冰球运动的综合技术
Chapter Four　The Basic Technique of Floorball

Drill 11

Objective:

1) To practice passing and receiving in motion.

2) To teach awareness of all the players on the field.

Organization:

1) The players are divided into teams of three persons.

2) The court is divided into three sections.

3) If goals are used, however not necessary, they can be marked with cones.

4) It is preferable if the teams have different coloured vests.

Execution:

1) 3 vs. 3 game.

2) The player with the ball is not allowed to move, which will activate the players without the ball, who have to create passing lanes by moving to an open space.

常规训练11

训练目的：

1) 跑动过程中的传接球练习；

2) 关注到场上所有的队员。

训练安排：

1) 队员3人一组；

2) 场地分为3部分；

3) 若使用球门，(尽管不必要) 仍应用锥形标识标示出；

4) 不同组别穿不同颜色比赛背心效果更好。

训练步骤：

1) 3打3对抗；

2) 持球队员不允许跑动，以此激发非持球队员跑动创造空档，制造传球路线；

北欧时尚运动——旱地冰球
Nordic Fashion Sport FLOORBALL

3)A team is supposed to keep the possession of the ball as long as possible and the passes are counted.

4)The team with more passes after 60 to 90 seconds is the winner.

5)The player with the ball has to make a pass in three seconds after receiving the ball.

6)If the opponent gains the possession of the ball, the roles will automatically switch.

7)The teams can rotate after one switch so that the winning team stays on the court and the loser moves on to the next court.

8)The winner of the whole tournament is therefore the team that has stayed on the same court the longest period of time.

Modifications:

1)Different rules can be added.

2)Players are only allowed to pass forward.

3）一方应尽可能长时间控球，传球数量纳入计算；

4）60－90秒后传球数量多的一方获胜；

5）持球队员在接球后3秒内必须传球给队友；

6）若对手控球，位置自动互换；

7）交换位置后可以进行轮转，进而获胜队可停留在原场地，失败队移到下一场地；

8）在同一场地停留时间最长的队伍是整场比赛的获胜队。

说明：

1）可添加不同规则；

2）队员只能向前传球；

第四章 旱地冰球运动的综合技术
Chapter Four　The Basic Technique of Floorball

3)Emphasizes the fact that there is actually only one passing opportunity because there should always be one player behind the ball carrier, similar to a defender during a game and this player cannot be passed to.

4)The leveling of the offensive team is crucial.

5)Emphasis on attacking, Only one time passes allowed.

6)Emphasizes the quick reaction and fast speed.

7)Only for very advanced players with good passing skills.

Key points:

1)Readiness to pass and receive a pass.

2)Head up.

3)Non-ball carriers have to move to create passing lanes and not stay behind the opponent (passing shade).

4)Rules should be strictly followed and equal.

3) 强调传球机会只有一次，因为持球队员身后总有一个队员（类似于防守方），但不能传球给他；

4) 进攻方的部署至关重要；

5) 强调进攻，只允许一次传球；

6) 强调快速反应以及快速跑动；

7) 此训练只适用于有高超传球技巧的球员。

训练要点：

1) 随时准备传接球；

2) 抬头；

3) 非持球队员需通过跑动创造传球线路，而不是站在对手身后（传球路线会被挡住）；

4) 严格遵循规则，确保公平。

Drill 12

Objective:

1) To practice passing and receiving in game like situations; openings.

2) To take the individual techniques into game performance.

3) To practice the movement in the chosen opening.

Organization:

1) The players can be divided either by their playing positions (defenders, wings, centre forwards) or can be switched so that every player has to play each position (preferable for the beginners).

2) The coach gives the players the positions where to start depending on the way the team wants to open up the play.

Execution:

1) Two defenders (A1 and A2) on the corner face-off dot giving a hit-in.

常规训练12

训练目的：

1) 如正式比赛中的传接球训练，开球；

2) 将个人技术综合运用到比赛中；

3) 开球后的跑动训练。

训练安排：

1) 队员可由其自身所打位置（防守，边路，主攻）分类；或者调换角色，可以让每个球员有机会尝试不同的位置（特别适合初学者）；

2) 教练确定运动员从哪里开打，取决于团队开球方式。

训练步骤：

1) 2名防守队员(A1和A2)在争球点打进一个边线球；

第四章　旱地冰球运动的综合技术
Chapter Four　The Basic Technique of Floorball

2)Winger (A4) on the same side by the board, the centre forward (A3) in the centre few meters from the goal area and the top-striker (A5) either in front of the opponents goal or by the board on the same side with the pressure (strong side).

3)A1 passes the ball to A2 who has two options:

①To pass the ball to A4, who gives a one timer to A3, who continues to A5 who shoots.

②Move behind the goal and pass to A3, who has now moved to the strong side of the court, who gives a one timer to A4, while moving towards the offensive zone, A3 passes to A5 who can either pass to A4 or back to A3 ⋯⋯

2) 边路A4位于挡板附近，主攻A3在距球门附近数米的中场，射门球员A5以强大的攻势处于对方球门前或者在同一侧的挡板旁边；

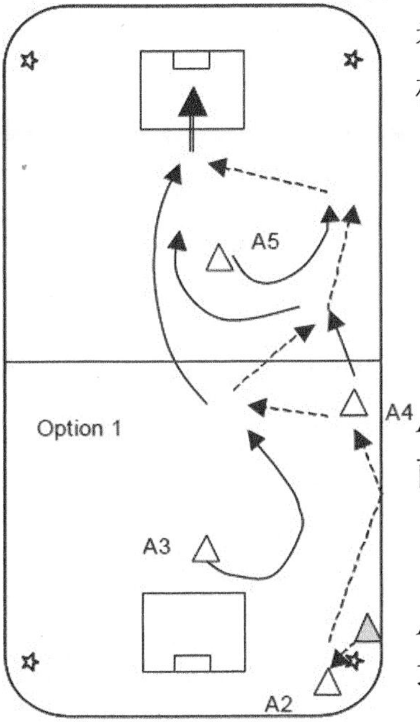

3) A1传球给A2，此时A2有两个选择：

①传球给A4，A4紧接着一传成功给A3，A3继续传球给A5，A5射门，

②从球门后运球将球传给A3，A3此时处于强势边路，A3可以一传成功给A4，当处于进攻区域时，A3将球传给A5，A5可以传给A4或是回传给A3⋯⋯

图4-11

· 103 ·

4) The defenders should also move to support the attack.

5) The attack should always end up with a shot.

6) One performance should not contain more than 5-6 passes.

7) After one performance the players switch positions (either A1 to A2, A2 to A3 etc, or the whole line-up).

Modifications:

1) Ways to start can be varied.

2) For example A1 and A2 passing to each other in front of the goal.

3) If the team is practicing libero play, the game is opened by using a low triangle (A1, A2 and A4).

4) 防守队员应跑位来帮助进攻；

5) 进攻队员每次都应以射门结束进攻；

6) 一轮传球不得超过5—6次；

7) 一轮后各球员轮换位置（A1变到A2，A2变到A3等等，或者整组轮换）。

图4-12

说明：

1) 开始的方式可以变换；

2) 例如，A1和A2在球门前互相传球；

3) 若球队在练习自由打法，则比赛可以以小角度开球(A1, A2 和 A4)；

第四章 旱地冰球运动的综合技术
Chapter Four   The Basic Technique of Floorball

4)In the beginning this should be executed without an opponent, but then adding the defensive team makes the play more game like and difficult.

5)If there are less players the drill can be executed in only one end.

6)After opening the play, the forwards (A3, A4, A5) have to go around a cone (or the opposite goal), regroup and attack against A1 and A2.

Key Points:

1)The main emphasis is on the passes and timing.

2)Passing and receiving while moving.

3)Head up. Ready to pass and receive and repractice so that the players are only passing the ball without movement (figure 4-13).

4) 开始时不设置对手球队，之后加入防守球队可以使整个训练增加难度系数、更加像比赛；

5) 如果队员人数不够，训练可以在一个半场进行；

6) 比赛开始后，前锋（A3,A4,A5）需绕锥形标（或对方球门），重新组队，且进攻对抗A1、A2一方。

训练要点：

1) 训练重点在于传球和把握时间；

2) 跑动时传接球；

3) 抬头，做好传球和接球的准备。球员传球时不需跑动（图4-13）。

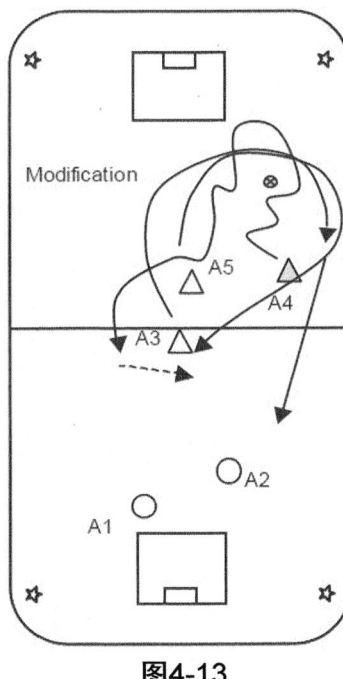

图4-13

Drill 13

Objective:

1) To practice passing and receiving while moving: finishing attacks.

2) To transfer individual skills into game performance.

3) To practice moving in the offensive zone and scoring.

Organization:

1) Players are divided as in drill 12.

2) A defensive team can be added without sticks or by playing with sticks upside down.

3) A defensive team can also be simulated by cones in the beginning (as figure 4-14) to emphasiz the passing with the attacking team.

4) In the beginning, and especially with young players, the passing lanes can be practiced so

常规训练13

训练目的:

1) 跑动过程中的传接球练习：完成进攻；

2) 将个人技术综合运用到比赛中；

3) 练习进攻区域内跑动和射门。

训练安排:

1) 队员按照练习12中的要求进行分组；

2) 可以加入防守方，无杆或杆朝下进行防守；

3) 开始训练时用锥形标代替进攻方可以让防守方更易进入状态（如图4-14），以加强训练有进攻方时的传球；

4) 训练初期，尤其是年轻队员应当反复练习并熟悉传球线路，进而队员可以不

第四章 旱地冰球运动的综合技术
Chapter Four   The Basic Technique of Floorball

that the players are only passing the ball without movement (figure 4-14).

5)The coach should also make clear before starting where the defensive team is situated, and bring out the best options for the attacking teams players' where to be open for a pass and where are the best places to score by using the tactic board (opponent covering the best scoring sector as figure 4-15 shows).

需要跑动而传球（图4-14）；

5) 训练前教练应当对防守队员各自的站位进行讲解，利用战术图给进攻队提供最好的传球路线和得分选择（如图4-15所示，对方占据着最佳射门区域）。

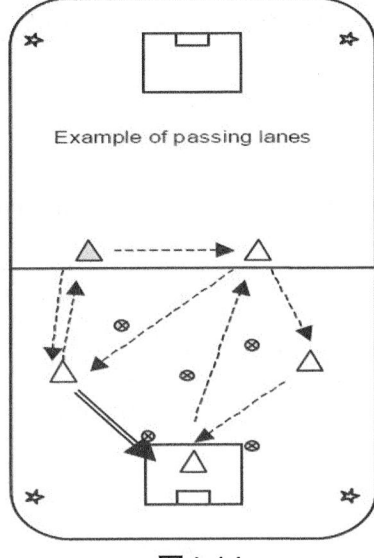

图4-14

Execution:

1)A1 and A2 are giving a free-hit by the middle line (figure 4-15).

2)A3 is situated near the rink, A4 in the middle and A5 on the offensive corner on the strong side of the rink.

训练步骤：

1) A1和A2在中线处打一个任意球（图4-15）；

2) A3在靠近场边的地方，A4在中场，A5在进攻区的密集侧翼；

3) The forwards can also switch places, in floorball the positions are not designated, especially in the offensive play and the players are encouraged to be creative in attacking situations.

4) The ball is passed around with the players first still standing.

3) 前锋可以轮换位置，在旱地冰球运动中位置不是预先设定的，尤其是在进攻时，队员需要自己创造适合的进攻机会；

4) 球由首先站好位的队员开始传。

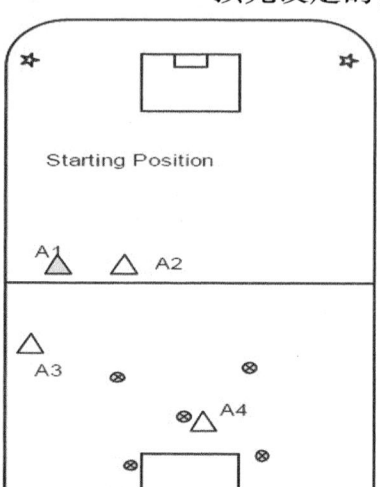

图4-15

The movement:

1) If A1 and A2 are passing to each other (figure 4-15) the forwards should move to open spaces (depending on the placed cones, or the opponent) ready to receive a pass.

2) If in libero play (figure 4-16) the ball is played to the left side to winger A3, A5 moves to the corner on the left side and

跑位：

1) 如果A1和A2互相传球（图4-15），前锋应该跑向空档位置（根据锥形标或防守方的位置），做好接球的准备；

2) 如果训练是自由模式（图4-16），球要传给边路位置的A3，A5跑到靠近中场的左侧位置，A4跑到中心

第四章 旱地冰球运动的综合技术
Chapter Four　The Basic Technique of Floorball

A4 moves closer to the centre (either behind or in front of the goal depending on the opponents moves).

3)The attack should end with a shot after 5-6 passes.

4)The same passing figure can be repeated as many times as necessary until the players have understood and remembered the figure, and other variations can be added (also using the creativity of the players themselves).

5)After three to four attacks either the positions or the whole line-up should be switched.

Modifications:

1)Can be modified by changing the number of defensive players (also 5 against 4).

（根据防守方移动情况，跑位到球门前或后）；

3) 在5-6次传球后必须射门完成进攻；

4) 同一传球模式可重复训练多次，直到队员理解且记住这一模式，同样，训练也可以变换形式（发挥队员的创造力）；

5) 3-4次进攻后，球员交换位置，或者全队进行整体轮换。

说明：

1)可变换防守方的球员人数（5打4也可以）；

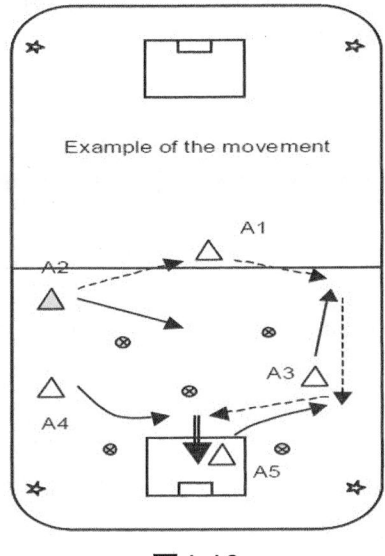

图4-16

2)Also the figure of passing can be modified depending on the chosen play system (using the centre or the corners).

Key Points:

1)Using the open space, avoiding dangerous passes and poor scoring zones.

2)Readiness to pass and receive.

3)Head up.

4)Players should be encouraged to also use their own creativity.

5)The level of the players should be considered.

2) 根据选用的训练方式，传球模式也可以改变（利用好中场或者死角）。

训练要点：

1) 利用好空档位置，避免不利的传球，避开射门几率较小的区域；

2) 随时准备传接球；

3) 抬头；

4) 鼓励队员发挥创造力；

5) 充分考虑队员的能力水平。

中国旱地冰球信息网 www.floorballinfo.com
国际旱地冰球联合会 www.floorball.org

第四章 旱地冰球运动的综合技术
Chapter Four　The Basic Technique of Floorball

Drill 14

Objective:

1) To practice passing in the offensive zone.

2) To practice creating space in opening and finishing attacks.

3) To practice timing of passing and moving.

Organization:

1) A1 behind the goal.

2) A3 at the middle line near the rink.

3) A2 in the other corner with the rest of the players and balls.

4) The coach should make the objective of timing the passes and movement clear beforehand.

常规训练14

训练目的：

1) 进攻区域的传球训练；

2) 在开始或结束进攻时创造跑位的训练；

3) 传接球和跑动计时练习。

训练安排：

1) A1站在球门后；

2) A3在靠近场边的中线处；

3) A2与其他队员在另一个角落；

4) 教练应提前告知队员传球和跑动的计时目标。

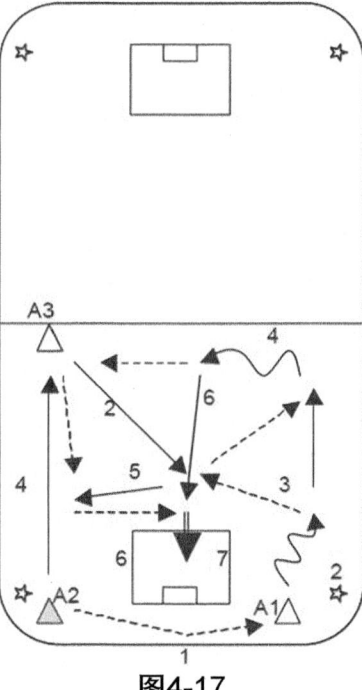

图4-17

北欧时尚运动——旱地冰球
Nordic Fashion Sport FLOORBALL

Execution:

1)First part demonstrates an opening in the defensive zone.

2)A1 starts running towards the corner while receiving a pass from A2.

3)A1 continues running by the board while A3 moves to the centre.

4)A1 passes a one-timer to A3 and continues running towards the middle line, the second part demonstrates an attack in the defensive zone.

5)A1 continues following the middle line, while A2 runs by the board towards the line (after the first pass), A2 receives a pass from A1.

6)A3 waits in the slot, as in game like situation, prepared to receive a pass, but as A1 passes to A2, A3 moves by the board to receive a pass from A2.

7)A1 runs towards the slot to receive a pass from A3, A1 shoots.

训练步骤：

1) 首先防守区开球；

2) A1向角落处跑，同时接A2的传球；

3) A1沿隔球板跑动，同时A3向中场跑；

4) A1向A3一次传球后继续向中线跑动，第二部分体现防守区域的进攻；

5) A1继续沿中线跑动，同时，A2沿隔球板跑向中线（第一次传球后），A2接A1的传球；

6) 和真实比赛一样，A3在射门有利区等候接球，但当A1传球给了A2，A3沿隔球板跑动接A2的传球；

7) A1向射门有利区跑动，接A3传球，A1射门；

第四章 旱地冰球运动的综合技术
Chapter Four The Basic Technique of Floorball

8) A1 becomes A2, A2 becomes A3 and A3 becomes A1.

8) A1变成A2，A2变成A3，A3变成A1。

中国旱地冰球信息网 www.floorballinfo.com
国际旱地冰球联合会 www.floorball.org

2. Shooting

Level 1

Drill 15

Objective:

1) To practice different techniques of shooting.

2) To learn to keep the head up when shooting.

3) To learn the right grip and posture.

4) Warm up the goalkeeper.

Organization:

1) Players are standing on a half circle from about eight meters from the goal with one ball each.

2) Players should keep distance to each other and give room for the player next to shoot.

2.射门

第一阶段

常规训练 15

训练目的:

1) 练习不同的射门技巧;

2) 练习射门时保持抬头;

3) 练习正确握杆和姿势;

4) 守门员热身。

训练安排:

1) 每位球员持球分别站在距离球门8米的半圆之内;

2) 球员之间应当保持距离,且给身旁球员足够的射门空间。

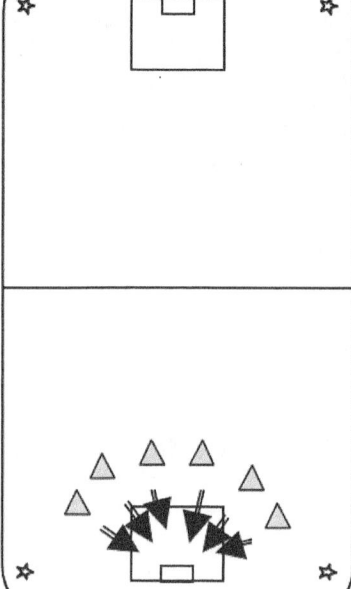

图4-18

第四章 旱地冰球运动的综合技术
Chapter Four　The Basic Technique of Floorball

Execution:

1)Players start one by one from the other end of the line to shoot towards the goal.

2)Different shots used.

3)First easy shots for the goalkeeper to catch (wrist shot).

4)When the goalkeeper is getting warm, more power can be used (slap shot).

Modifications:

1)To get the goalkeeper moving sideways, the shooters are alternated from side to side.

2)To shoot while moving the players can take two steps towards the goal before the shot (otherwise same order).

3)To get more repetitions, or with less players the players can shoot 3-4 balls at the same turn.

训练步骤:

1) 球员从队伍另一端开始,依次射门;

2) 不同的射门方式;

3) 首先练习守门员最容易防守的球(抖腕射门);

4) 守门员热身结束,渐渐进入状态后,可以加大射门力度(击射)。

说明:

1) 使守门员向球门边运动,射手需要不断跑动变换跑位;

2) 在跑动射门的过程中,球员可以向球门移动两步然后射门(其他情况顺序一样);

3) 为更多重复练习,或者球员人数较少,球员一轮可以用3—4个球射门。

Key points:

1) Head up.

2) Right posture and grip.

3) Give space for the next shooter.

4) The players should be ordered to collect the balls quickly after one round to able the next round as fast as possible.

5) If children are involved, they should be advised not to collect the balls from the goal or behind the goal until everybody has taken their shot to avoid injury.

训练要点：

1) 保持抬头；

2) 正确的姿势和握杆方法；

3) 给下一个射手留出空间；

4) 一轮结束后，球员应当及时捡球，以便下一轮尽快开始；

5) 如果有儿童参与，为避免受伤，确保每个射手都完成射门训练后，才可以从球门或球门后捡球。

第四章 旱地冰球运动的综合技术
Chapter Four The Basic Technique of Floorball

Drill 16

Objective:

1) To practice shooting from different angles and positions.

2) Warm up for the goalkeepers.

Organization:

1) One player standing in front of the goal in a game like position (A1).

2) Other players are standing in half circle with one ball each ready to pass.

Execution:

1) The players start to pass the ball to A1 one at a time in order (either proceeding from the other side or alternating the sides).

2) A1 tries to shoot straight from the pass no matter which side or where the ball is passed to.

3) After shooting A1 moves to the line and the next player from the line takes the shots.

常规训练 16

训练目的：

1) 不同角度不同位置的射门训练；

2) 守门员的热身训练。

训练安排：

1) 如同正式比赛，一名球员站在球门前 (A1)；

2) 其他球员站在半圆区域，每人持一球，准备传球。

训练步骤：

1) 球员（一次一个）依次给A1传球（从一侧或变换方向皆可）；

2) 不论球是从哪个边线过来，或是球传向哪里，A1接球后需尽力直接射门；

3) 射门后，A1返回队列，队中下一位队员射门。

北欧时尚运动——旱地冰球
Nordic Fashion Sport FLOORBALL

Modifications:

1)Also aerial passes so the player who is shooting has to practice ball-eye coordination as well.

2)For more advanced players, one more pass can be added so that the player who is supposed to give the pass to A1, gives a pass to some other player on the line, who then passes the ball to A1. This way, A1 cannot predict from where the pass comes but has to react to the pass and position him/herself to shoot quickly.

Key points:

1)Players should be ready to pass and shoot.

2)Right grip according to the shot.

3)Game like position (knees bent, low posture).

说明:

1) 同时,可以加入空中传球,这样射门队员就能够练习球眼协调;

2) 对于进阶球员来说可以再加入一个传接球训练,也就是说:原本应该传球给A1的球员,此时把球传给队列中的其他球员,然后这一名队员再传球给A1,这样,A1无法预测球从哪里传来,但是必须很快做出反应,并马上射门。

训练要点:

1) 球员应随时准备传接球和射门;

2) 根据射门方式正确握杆;

3) 正式比赛站姿(屈膝低位)。

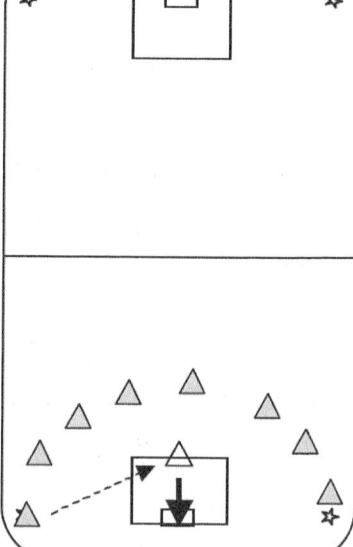

图4-19

第四章 旱地冰球运动的综合技术
Chapter Four The Basic Technique of Floorball

Drill 17

Objective:

1) To practice different type of shots.

2) To practice shooting while moving.

3) Warm-up for the goal-keeper.

Organization:

1) Players form three lines by the middle line with balls.

2) Cones in the corners.

Execution:

1) One player from each line takes a shot at a time.

2) Different shots from different lines.

3) A short wrist shot.

4) Wrist shot with a long back drive.

5) Penalty shot, the order will force the goalkeeper to move sideways.

常规训练 17

训练目的：

1) 训练不同种类的射门；

2) 训练跑动过程中的射门；

3) 守门员热身。

训练安排：

1) 球员持球分三列站在中线附近；

2) 底角用三角锥标示。

训练步骤：

1) 每次每列出一名队员射门；

2) 不同列进行不同种类的射门训练；

3) 短距离抖腕射门；

4) 长后推力的抖腕射门；

5) 罚球，目的是强制守门员练习横向移动。

6) After the shot, players have to go around the cone in the opposite corner so that a movement forward will follow the shot and that the players won't stay in front of the next shooter.

7) The player from the middle line has to go around the goal-cage.

8) The lines will rotate in clockwise order.

Modifications:

1) Shots can be varied.

2) Also lines can be added in the corners, from where the player has to shoot a wrist shot from protection or a backhand shot.

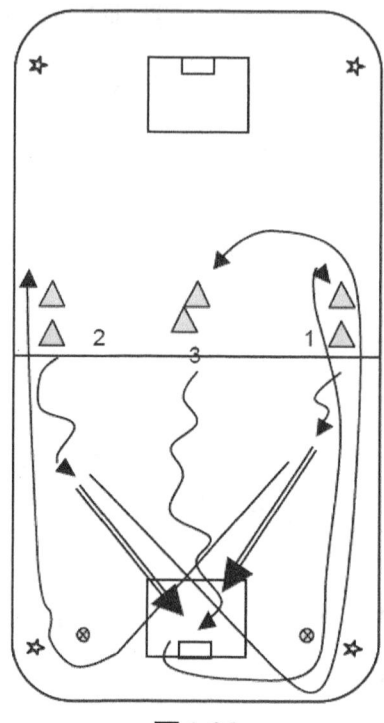

图4-20

6) 射门后，球员需要到对面底角绕过三角锥，这样一来射门后可以有下一轮的进攻跟进，球员也不会挡到下一位射手；

7) 中线处的球员需绕球门跑动；

8) 各列按照顺时针轮换。

说明：

1) 射门方式可以变化；

2) 同时，底角处可加入一列球员，这里可进行抖腕射门或者反手挥杆射门；

第四章 旱地冰球运动的综合技术
Chapter Four   The Basic Technique of Floorball

3)One timer can also be added so that the player from the line on the left side passes a one timer to the player in the middle line, receives the pass back and shoots a one timer.

Key points:

1)Right grip according to the shot.

2)Players should be encouraged to follow the movement forward after the shot.

3)Players should not stay in front of the next shooter.

4)Players should wait so that the goalkeeper is ready to receive the next shot.

5)Players from lines 1 and 2 should not go too close to the goal, however the shot should be accurate rather than hard to warm up the goalkeeper.

6)Harder shots can be taken once the goalkeeper has been warmed up.

3)训练中可以加入一轮传球，这样球场左侧球员可以传一次性球给中线处的球员，然后接回传射门。

训练要点：

1) 按照射门方式运用正确的握杆方法；

2) 射门后，鼓励球员跟进进攻；

3) 球员不能站在下一位射手前；

4) 球员等待守门员准备好接下一个球再射门；

5) 第一列和第二列的球员离球门不要太近，但是射门务必准确，否则守门员状态预热不够；

6) 当守门员进入状态后，可以进行更高难度的射门。

Drill 18

Objective:

1) To practice shooting while moving.

2) Warm up for the goalkeeper.

3) To practice sideway movement for the goalkeeper.

Organization:

1) Players form two lines by the middle line facing the goal with balls.

2) For beginners there can be cones added to mark the shooting spots.

Execution:

1) A1 starts running by the rink angling towards the goal.

2) To get the goalkeeper moving sideways, the player should clearly cross the middle sector before shooting.

3) After shooting, the players continues to the line on the other side to shoot alternately from

常规训练 18

训练目的:

1) 练习跑动过程中的射门;

2) 守门员热身训练;

3) 守门员侧移练习。

训练安排:

1) 球员持球面向球门,在中线两侧分成两列;

2) 对初学者来说可以加入三角锥作为射门点的标示。

训练步骤:

1) A1开始沿面向球门的角度跑动;

2) 为使守门员侧移,队员射门前务必穿过球场中场;

3) 射门后,球员继续跑动至中线另一边,交叉正反

第四章　旱地冰球运动的综合技术
Chapter Four　The Basic Technique of Floorball

forehand and backhand side.

手位射门。

Modifications:

说明：

1)The players can also start from the corners so that the shots will be shot from protection.

1) 球员亦可从底角处开始跑动，防护紧密时射门；

2)In another variation, the players can start from the corners and shoot after the opposite sides cone.

2) 其他训练模式如，球员可以从底角出发，从球场另一侧的三角锥标示处射门。

Key points:

训练要点：

1)Right grip and posture.

1) 正确的握杆方式和姿势；

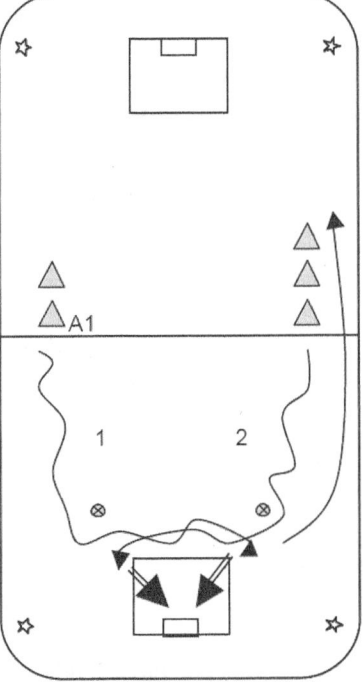

图4-21

2)Shooting from good protection.

2) 严密防护球到时射门；

3)The goalkeeper should follow the shooters movement, not predict the shot or position him/herself already on the other corner of the goal (simulates game play for the goalkeeper).

3) 守门员要随着射手跑动而移动，不要预测射门，也不要把射手定位在球门另一角（为守门员进行模拟比赛场景训练）。

Drill 19

Objective:

1) To practice shooting while moving.

2) To practice direct shot from a pass.

3) Warm-up drill for the goalkeeper.

Organization:

1) Players form two lines in the corners with balls.

2) Two cones about three meters from the rink near the middle line to mark the turning point for the players (especially beginners).

Execution:

1) A1 starts running by the rink towards the cone without a ball, runs around the cone and makes a fast turn facing the goal.

2) After the turn the player receives a pass from the opposite corner (B1).

常规训练 19

训练目的:

1) 训练跑动中的射门;

2) 训练传接球后直接射门;

3) 守门员热身训练。

训练安排:

1) 球员分两列,持球站在底角处;

2) 距离中线三米的边线处放置两个三角锥,以便为球员(尤其是新手)提供转回标示处。

训练步骤:

1) A1不持球,面向三角锥开始跑动,绕三角锥一圈,继而快速转身面向球门;

2) 转身后球员从对面底角B1处接球;

第四章 旱地冰球运动的综合技术
Chapter Four　The Basic Technique of Floorball

3)The player can either take control of the ball and then shoot (beginners) or shoot direct from the pass which demands good timing and eye-ball coordination.

3) 球员接球后可以先稳好球然后射门（初学者）；对来球时机判断准确、眼与球调控得当的球员，可接球后直接射门；

4)After the shot A1 moves to the other corner.

4) 射门后A1向另一个底角跑动；

5)B1 executes the same, receiving a pass from the opposite corner (A2).

5) B1的训练路线如上，从对面底角A2处接球；

6)For beginners, the pass can be made standing still, but as soon as possible, the players should be encouraged to pass while moving, also this helps to speed up the drill.

6) 对于初学者来说，球员可以站定接球，但是应鼓励球员尽量在跑动中传球，这样有助于加快训练进程；

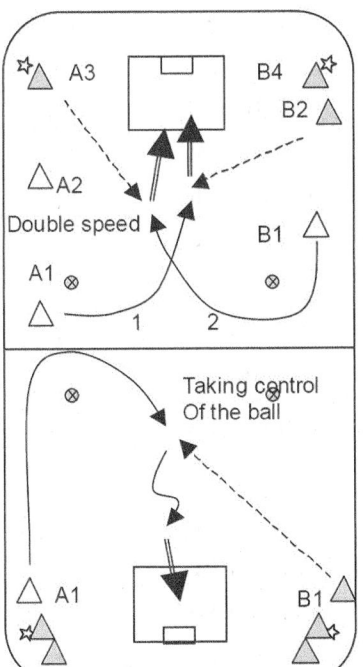

7)It is better to start with a wrist shot and then move on to different shots.

7) 最好由抖腕射门开始，然后进行不同类型的射门训练。

图4-22

北欧时尚运动——旱地冰球
Nordic Fashion Sport FLOORBALL

Modifications:

1) The coach can determine whether he/she wants the shot to be direct or not.

2) If the shot is direct, the pass should be aimed closer to the goal, and if the player is supposed to take control of the ball first, the pass should be aimed further away from the goal.

3) The ball can also be passed from the same line, that is from behind, which will emphasize the ball control when the player has to receive the ball from behind and dribble around the cone before the shot.

4) Also aerial passes to emphasize the receiving a lifted ball which can happen during a game.

5) When the players are familiar with the drill, it can be executed with double speed so that A1, A2 and B1 are all running before the first ball is passed.

说明:

1) 教练可以决定接球后是否立即射门;

2) 如果接球后立即射门,传球应在球门附近区域进行;如果球员需要先稳住球,传球应在远离球门的区域进行;

3) 也可以选择在同一线(即从后面)传球,接后面的传球要让球员知道控球的重要性,在三角锥附近运球,然后射门;

4) 球员要清楚比赛中可能出现空中传球,强调接这类球的重要性;

5) 球员更加熟悉此类训练后,可以双倍速度进行,这样一来,传第一个球前,A1,A2和B1都在跑动;

第四章　旱地冰球运动的综合技术
Chapter Four　The Basic Technique of Floorball

6)In this case B2 passes the ball to A1 and A3 passes to B1 and B4 to A2.

Key points:

1)The ball should be passed while moving to keep up and increase the speed.

2)Head should always be lifted up before the shot.

3)Accurate passes (the player shooting should point out where he/she wants the pass) with correct speed.

4)Timing of the pass, not too early or too late, attacking player and the ball must meet at the same point at the same time.

5)It is always good to start with ball control first, and then move forward to direct shots.

6) 这种情况下B2传球给A1，A3传球给B1，B4传球给A2。

训练要点：

1) 跑动中传球以加快训练速度；

2) 射门前保持头部抬起；

3) 以适合速度精准传球（射门球员需要指出他/她希望获得传球的方位）；

4) 掌握传球时机，不早不晚，进攻球员要在同一时间、同一点获得传球；

5) 初学时，先训练控球是非常有效的，然后再继续其他直接射门训练。

中国旱地冰球信息网 www.floorballinfo.com
国际旱地冰球联合会 www.floorball.org

Nordic Fashion Sport FLOORBALL

Drill 20

Objective:

1) To practice shooting one timers and directing the ball.

2) To practice accurate shots from both ground and aerial passes.

3) Warm up for the goalkeeper (sideways movement).

Organization:

Players form two lines by the rink at the middle line with balls.

Execution:

1) A1 starts running towards the slot.

2) When A1 reaches the goal area, he/ she will receive a hard pass from A2.

3) A1 shoots an accurate shot, or more or less directs the ball towards the goal.

4) After the pass, A2 executes the same.

5) After the shot, players switch lines.

常规训练 20

训练目的：

1) 练习一次性射门，引导球的方向；

2) 练习地面和空中传球的精准射门；

3) 守门员热身(侧移运动)。

训练安排：

球员分两列持球站在中线处。

训练步骤：

1) A1向射门有利区域跑动；

2) A1靠近射门区域时，他/她会从A2处接到劲传；

3) A1准确射门进球，或至少也是构成对于球门的威胁；

4) 传球过后，A2进行相同的训练；

5) 射门后，球员互换。

第四章　旱地冰球运动的综合技术
Chapter Four　The Basic Technique of Floorball

Modifications:

Also aerial passes.

A1 can also run parallel with the middle line, receive a short pass from A2 and continue towards the goal performing a shoot out.

Key points:

1) The shot shouldn't be more than a directive touch with the ball(one time shot),both forehand and backhand should be used, and one hand grip should be used to reach the ball.

2) The player can also receive the pass with forehand and shoot with a backhand side, or vice versa depending on the situation.

说明：

空中传球；

A1可以平行中线跑动，从A2处接到短传球，继续跑向球门，发动射门。

训练要点：

1) 射门迅速，直接触球即射（一次射门）正手球和反手球都应使用，可单手握杆以便触到球；

2) 球员可以正手接球反手射门，或反之，依情况而定。

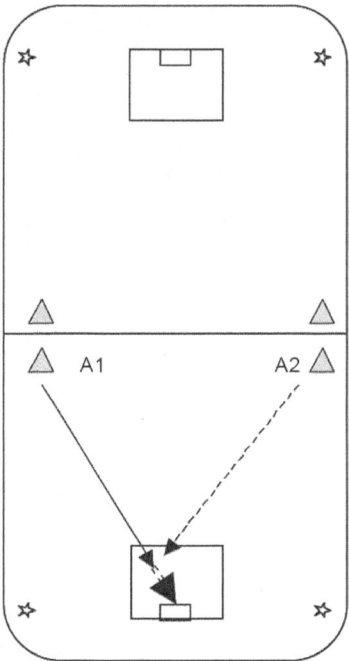

图4-23

• 129 •

Level 2

Drill 21

Objective:

1) To practice shooting from protection and while moving.

2) To practice timing of the shot.

3) To practice gaining space for a shot.

4) For the goalkeeper to practice sideways movement and saves at close distance.

Organization:

Players are in the corners with balls.

Execution:

1) A1 starts running towards the slot without a ball.

第二阶段

常规训练 21

训练目的:

1) 跑动过程中的射门或有防护时的射门;

2) 训练射门的及时性;

3) 寻找进球空间训练;

4) 守门员着重训练侧移运动和近距离防卫。

训练安排:

球员持球分布各底角。

训练步骤:

1) A1不带球,向射门有利区跑动;

第四章 旱地冰球运动的综合技术
Chapter Four The Basic Technique of Floorball

2)A2 starts running towards A1 with a ball when A1 has crossed the middle slot.

3)A2 gives a drop pass to A1 who shoots.

4)A2 continues running towards the opposite corner, now without a ball.

5)A3 leaves from the corner with a ball and gives a drop pass to A2, who shoots and so on.

6)After execution, the players switch lines to get a shot from the other side.

Modifications:

1)The coach can play a defender, harassing the players to emphasize the importance of the protection of the ball.

2)Close distance shots can

2) 当 A1 穿过射门区中场时，A2带球跑向 A1；

3) A2 传运传球给A1射门；

4) A2不带球，继续向对面底角跑动；

5) A3从底角带球跑动，传运传球给 A2，A2射门，以此类推；

6) 一轮过后，球员换列，在另一边射门。

说明：

1) 教练可以打后卫，不断提醒和强调护球的重要性；

2) 近距离射门也可以作

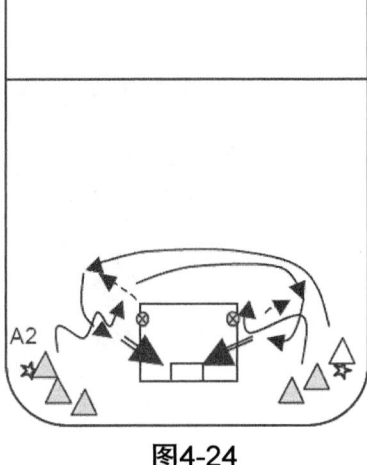

图4-24

北欧时尚运动——旱地冰球
Nordic Fashion Sport FLOORBALL

also be practiced as direct shots so that a pass is given from the opposite corner.

Key points:

The drop pass has to be accurate so that the opponent does not have time to intercept the pass.

为直接射门进行练习,这样传球从对面底角开始。

训练要点:

停运传球必须精准,这样才不会给对手时间断球。

Chapter Four The Basic Technique of Floorball

Drill 22

Objective:

1) To practice both close distance and long distance shots while moving.

2) To practice two men screen.

3) To practice aggressive play in the slot.

Organization:

1) Four lines: two in the corners and two at the middle line by the rink.

2) All lines facing the goal with balls.

3) The coach should emphasise the importance of the screen beforehand.

Execution:

1) A1 takes few steps from the corner and shoots from a small angle (short wrist shot, backhand).

2) A2 does the same from

常规训练 22

训练目的：

1) 训练跑动过程中的短距离、长距离射门；

2) 训练两人盯防；

3) 练习射门有利区的有效进攻。

训练安排：

1) 分为四列：两列在底角，两列在中线附近；

2) 所有队员持球面向球门；

3) 教练应提前强调掩护的重要性。

训练步骤：

1) A1从底角跑动数步，然后小角度射门（短线腕射，反手射）；

2) A2从另一个底角重复

the other corner.

3) After this both players move to the slot to screen the goalkeeper.

4) A3 takes few steps towards the middle dot and shoots a long distance shot (long wrist shot, forehand drive, slap shot).

5) A4 does the same.

6) After one round the players rotate in clockwise order.

Modifications:

1) A1 and A2 can also play one versus one situation in front of the goal, so that A1 is the offensive player and A2 is defensive.

2) A2 can also have the option to pass to A1 to shoot if

相同动作；

3) 上述动作结束后，两名球员一起跑动至射门有利区，干扰守门员视线；

4) A3数步跑动至中间点，长球射门（长距腕射，正手射，击射）；

5) A4重复上述步骤。

6) 一轮过后，球员们按照顺时针方向轮换。

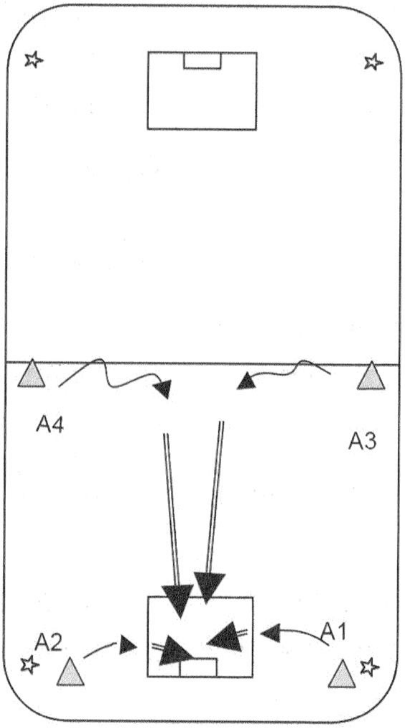

说明：

1) A1和A2也能在球门前进行一对一的对抗，A1是进攻方，A2是防守方；

2) 如果A1的射门条件更加有利，A2也可以传球给

图4-25

第四章　旱地冰球运动的综合技术
Chapter Four　The Basic Technique of Floorball

A1 has a better opportunity to score.

Key points:

1) Best way to screen the goalkeeper is to move, this way the goalkeeper also has to move and therefore it is harder for him/her to see the shot.

2) This is done so that the two screening players cross each other in front of the goalkeeper at the moment the shot is taken.

3) It is also better if at least one of the players is about one meter from the goalkeeper.

4) This way the screening player has time to turn around and hit the rebounds, even if the ball hits the player him/herself.

A1来射门。

训练要点：

1) 阻挡守门员最好的方法就是不断跑动，这样守门员也要不断跑动，这样他/她就更难看清楚球；

2) 射门时，两名阻挡守门员视线的球员交叉跑动；

3) 更理想的情况是进攻队中至少有一名球员距离守门员一米远；

4) 这样一来，即便是球打到球员身上，阻挡守门员视线的队员就有时间转身击回弹球。

Drill 23

Objective:

1) To practice a drop pass.

2) To practice a long distance shot.

3) To practice screening the goalkeeper and hitting rebounds.

Organization:

1) Players form two lines: one in the corner and one at the middle line by the rink.

2) Balls in the corner.

Execution:

1) A1 passes to A2.

2) A2 comes towards the pass and takes control of the ball.

3) A1 follows the pass and receives a drop pass from A2 when they cross.

4) A2 runs straight to the slot without looking back and A1 continues towards the middle spot with the ball.

5) As soon as A2 is ready to

常规训练 23

训练目的：

1) 练习停运传球；

2) 练习长距离射门；

3) 练习盯防守门员以及打回弹球。

训练安排：

1) 球员分两列站：一列在底角，另一列在中线处；

2) 球在底角。

训练步骤：

1) A1传球给A2；

2) A2迎球跑动继而控球；

3) A1随后，与A2相遇时获得停运传球；

4) A2不回视，径直向射门有利区跑动；A1继续带球向中场射门有利区跑动；

5) 一旦A2准备好盯防

第四章　旱地冰球运动的综合技术
Chapter Four　The Basic Technique of Floorball

screen the goalkeeper, A1 shoots a long distance shot (long wrist shot, slap shot, forehand drive).

6) A2 ready for rebounds.

7) After the execution players switch lines.

Modifications:

1) Defensive players can be added so that after the shot A1 plays a defender in front of the goal with the next screening player.

2) Also a defensive player can be added closer to the shooter to block the shot, which makes it harder for the shooter to aim the shot.

守门员，A1进行长球射门（长距腕射、击射、正手出击）；

6) A2随时准备打回弹球；

7) 训练一轮结束后双方换场地。

说明：

1) 可以加入防守队员，这样射门后A1和另一个盯防队员在球门前形成防守；

2) 同时可以在距射门球员更近的地方加上防守队员，可以使射门球员难以瞄准射门。

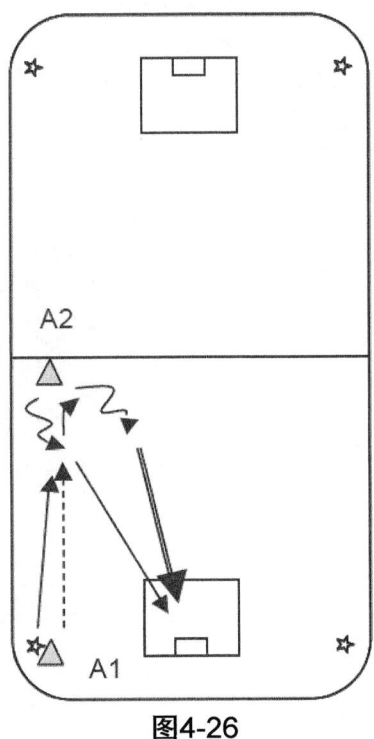

图4-26

北欧时尚运动——旱地冰球
Nordic Fashion Sport FLOORBALL

Key points:

1)The drop pass has to be accurate so that the opponent won't intercept the pass.

2)A2 should not follow A1 after the drop pass, but to continue straight to the slot.

3)The same main points in screening as in the previous drill.

训练要点：

1) 停运传球要准确，使对手没有机会拦截传球；

2) 停运传球后，A2应当直接跑动至射门有利区，而非跟随A1；

3) 盯防重点与前一训练一致。

第四章 旱地冰球运动的综合技术
Chapter Four　The Basic Technique of Floorball

Drill 24

Objective:

1) To practice scoring on two against zero.

2) To practice decision making; shoot or pass.

Organization:

Players in opposite corners with balls.

Execution:

1) A1 starts by running by the rink without a ball.

2) A1 receives a pass from A2.

3) They both run towards the middle line, A1 with the ball.

4) After crossing the middle line, A1 has to make a decision whether to give a drop

常规训练 24

训练目的：

1) 练习2对0进球；

2) 射门与否训练；射门或传球。

训练安排：

球员持球在对角处。

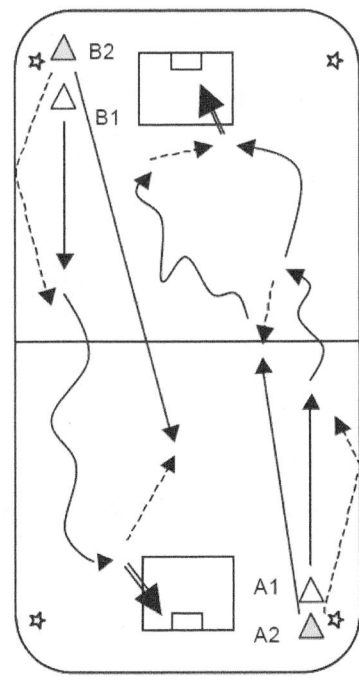

图4-27

训练步骤：

1) A1不带球沿球场跑动；

2) A1从A2处接球；

3) A1带球，二人都跑向中线；

4) 过中线后，A1需要做决定是传运传球给A2，然后自己继续前进到

pass to A2 and continue towards the opposite goal to screen the goalkeeper, or to continue running with the ball and shoot, or pass to A2 later.

5) B1 and B2 do the same at the same time.

6) After the execution, they move on to the opposite corner.

Modifications:

1) Also the goalkeeper can give the first pass to A1.

2) Other variations according to the coach, but the main emphasis should be on a quick finishing.

Key points:

1) Quick decision to finish the attack in a shot.

2) The players should leave at the same time from both corners.

对方球门前盯防守门；还是继续带球跑动射门，或者晚些传球给A2；

5) B1和B2同时进行同样的训练；

6) 经过训练后，他们跑动至对面底角。

说明：

1) 也可以是守门员传第一个球给A1；

2) 教练可以做其他的改变，但是重点应当还是快速完成射门。

训练要点：

1) 以射门结束进攻的果断性；

2) 两边底角球员应当同一时间开始跑动。

第四章 旱地冰球运动的综合技术
Chapter Four The Basic Technique of Floorball

Level 3

Drill 25

Objective:

1) To practice scoring.

2) To practice creating space for the ball carrier to shoot.

Organization:

1) One line by the rink at the middle line with balls.

2) Players A2 and A3 as in the figure 4-28.

3) Cones marking the opponent (can be replaced by real opponents).

4) The coach should make clear beforehand where the opponent is most likely to be situated.

5) This will help the players to avoid those areas.

Execution:

1) A1 passes the ball to A2 who comes towards the pass.

第三阶段

常规训练 25

训练目的：

1) 得分训练；

2) 为带球队员创造机会。

训练安排：

1) 中线处持球站成一排；

2) A2 与 A3 站位（如图 4-28）；

3) 以三角锥代表对手（可以换真人）；

4) 教练预先告知对手站位；

5) 这样有助于球员避免这些区域。

训练步骤：

1) A2迎球跑，A1传球给A2；

•141•

北欧时尚运动——旱地冰球
Nordic Fashion Sport FLOORBALL

2) A2 takes the ball under control and continues moving by the rink.

3) A1 starts moving towards the slot and receives a drop pass from A2 when they cross.

4) At the same time A3 moves from the centre towards the side creating space to the slot.

5) A1 moves towards the corner to a bad position to shoot so he/she passes to A3.

2) A2控球,继续沿球场跑动;

3) A1此时跑向有利射门区域,相遇时 A1接A2传来的停运传球;

4) 同时,A3从中场跑向边位寻找空位;

5) A1跑动至底角不利的射门位置,于是他/她传球给A3;

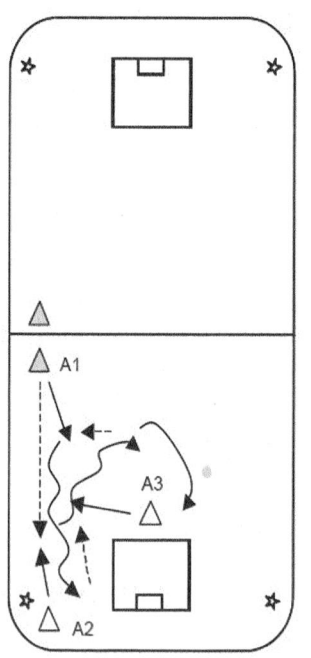
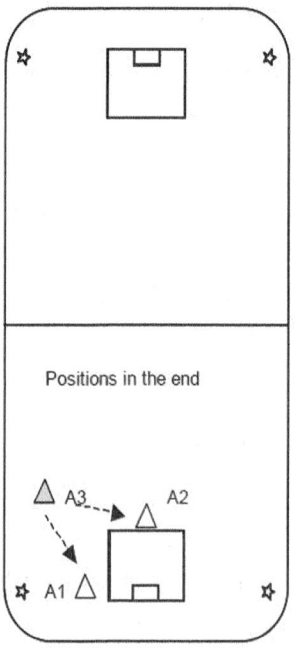

图4-28

第四章　旱地冰球运动的综合技术
Chapter Four　The Basic Technique of Floorball

6)A1 by the near post and A2 in front of the goal are open for a pass from A3 and ready to shoot.

7)After execution A1 becomes A2, A2 becomes A3 and A3 becomes A1.

Modifications:

1)The best way to modify the drill is to add defensive players to make it more difficult for the offensive team to score.

2)Also other variations of the passing figure and shooting positions can be made.

Key points:

1)Accurate shots should be emphasized.

2)A3 should quickly decide whom to pass to and A1 and A2 should be ready to shoot.

3)The movement of the players should be fast and the timing precise.

6) A1在门柱附近，A2在门前，二人随时可接受 A3 的传球，然后射门；

7) 一轮后，A1变成 A2，A2变成 A3，A3变成 A1。

说明：

1) 修改此训练的最佳途径是增加防守队的球员数，使进攻队更加难以得分；

2) 还可以有其他变化，例如传球方式和射门位置可以发生变化。

训练要点：

1) 重点练习精准进球；

2) A3应马上决定传球给A1还是A2，A1／A2应随时准备射门；

3) 球员跑动迅速，时机精确。

Nordic Fashion Sport FLOORBALL

Drill 26

Objective:

1)To practice scoring from tight situation.

2)To practice ball protection and fakes.

Organization:

1)Goal cages turned toward the corners about 7 meters from the boards (cones marking the area).

2)Balls on top of the goal.

3)Players divided in four even groups, if two goals (depending on the amount of players and goalkeepers).

4)Two groups forming two different lines on both sides of the goals.

Execution:

1)Goalkeeper throws a ball to the corner.

2)A1 and O1 fight for the ball.Whoever gets the posse-

常规训练 26

训练目的:

1) 紧张境况下进球;

2) 练习护球和假动作。

训练安排:

1) 球门朝向底角,相距底线7米(用三角锥围成);

2) 球在门上;

3) 如果有两个球门(取决于球员和守门员人数)球员分成四个偶数组;

4) 两组形成不同列,分站球门两边。

训练步骤:

1) 守门员将球扔至底角;

2) A1 与O1争抢球,得到球的球员变成攻击方,想

第四章　旱地冰球运动的综合技术
Chapter Four　The Basic Technique of Floorball

ssion becomes attacker and tries to shoot.

3) If the ball is hit of boundaries, if there is a score or a save, the goalkeeper throws in another ball.

4) 45 second shifts, players switch when the coach whistle.

Modifications:

1) After 45 seconds, two other players can be added, so that every other shift is played two versus two.

2) The aim is to shoot and for the other offensive player to get open to a place to shoot a one timer.

办法进球;

3) 如果球出界、进球或守门成功，守门员重新开球;

4) 45秒轮换一次，教练吹哨，球员换位。

说明：

1) 45秒后，可以加入其他两名队员，所以每次轮换就有一个二对二比赛；

2) 目标即进球，另外的防守队员开辟空位一击射门。

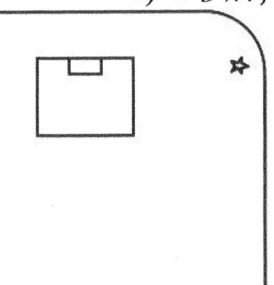

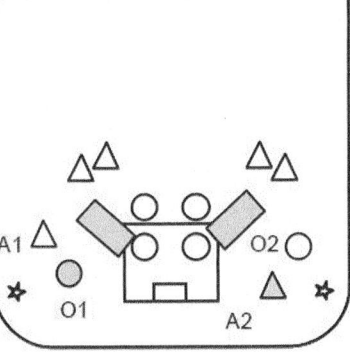

图4-29

Key points:

1) To emphasize shooting and protecting the ball.

2) Shoot when there is even a slight chance to score.

3) If there is no space to shoot, move or pass if possible.

4) Encourage the players to turn around and challenge the opponent.

训练要点:

1) 着重训练射门和防护;

2) 练习得分机会很小情况下的射门;

3) 如没有空位射门,尽可能跑动或传球;

4) 鼓励球员转身运球和挑战对手。

中国旱地冰球信息网 www.floorballinfo.com
国际旱地冰球联合会 www.floorball.org

第四章 旱地冰球运动的综合技术
Chapter Four The Basic Technique of Floorball

Drill 27

Objective:

1) To practice shooting and gaining a chance to shoot.

2) To practice game reading and decision making.

Organization:

1) Players are divided in groups of three or four.

2) The court is divided in half.

3) If four players in each group, one player is situated by the middle line as a stationary substitute player.

Execution:

1) Teams are playing three against three.

2) If a team with the ball (offensive) loses the ball either by: scoring, or the defensive team steals the ball or intercepts, the ball is hit out of boundaries, then the defensive team has to pass to

常规训练 27

训练目的：

1) 练习射门及寻找射门机会；

2) 练习赛情研判和决策能力。

训练安排：

1) 球员三人或四人为一组；

2) 场地一分为二；

3) 如果一组四人，则一名球员站中线处作为固定替补球员。

训练步骤：

1) 比赛实行三对三对抗；

2) 如果带球队（进攻方）因得分、对手偷球或拦截成功、球出界等方式失球，则进攻前，防守队员中丢球的队员应传球给固定/替

the stationary/substitute player before starting an attack and the player from the offensive team who lost the ball, has to switch with their stationary player.

3)The stationary/substitute player can move sideways to receive, pass and shoot.

4)If the stationary/substitute player is passed to other than after interception, the player has to shoot (demonstrating a defender shooting from the middle line).

5)In this case the closest player to the goal has to be ready to screen the goalkeeper.

Modifications:

1)Only one timer allowed.

2)There has to be a shot after three passes.

补球员，以此轮换；

3) 固定/替补球员可以跑动至侧面接球，传球和射门；

4) 如果球没有被拦截，固定/替补球员接到球，那么他必须射门（中线防守队员射门）；

5) 这种情况下，离球门最近的队员应当随时准备盯防守门员。

说明：

1) 只允许一击射门；

2) 三次传球后必须射门。

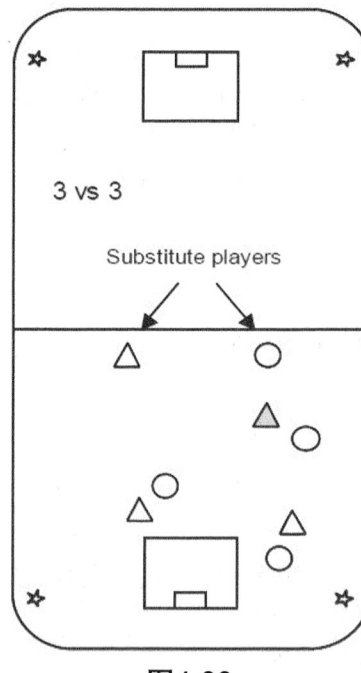

图4-30

第四章　旱地冰球运动的综合技术
Chapter Four　The Basic Technique of Floorball

Key points:

1) Players have to keep moving constantly and shoot whenever possible.

2) Players have to be ready to screen the goalie when the defender has the ball.

3) A player has to switch after losing the ball.

4) The rules should be strictly followed.

训练要点：

1) 球员需持续跑动，在任何适当时机射门；

2) 后卫控球后，球员需盯防守门员；

3) 球员丢球后，应当与中线处固定/替补球员互换位置；

4) 规则务必严格执行。

Drill 28

Objective:

1) To practice scoring as a part of team play.

2) To practice all the components from previous drills together.

3) For the defending team to practice a specific defensive game like formation.

Organization:

1) Players are divided in groups of five, or according to the teams line-ups.

2) The scrimmage is played five versus five on the offensive zone and the defending team is playing without sticks.

Execution:

1) A defender of the offensive team has the possession of the ball near the middle line.

2) The offensive team can play with both using the libero or using defender-defender pass.

常规训练 28

训练目的:

1) 练习球队配合得分;

2) 上述所有常规训练项目的整合练习;

3) 防守队练习比赛时特定防卫队形站位。

训练安排:

1) 球员按每组五人分组,或根据球员队列顺序;

2) 球员在进攻区域五对五争球练习,防守队不持杆。

训练步骤:

1) 在中线附近,进攻队的后卫持球;

2) 进攻队既可以使用自由后卫,也可以使用后卫—后卫传球;

第四章 旱地冰球运动的综合技术
Chapter Four The Basic Technique of Floorball

3) The wingers and the centre forward/top-striker are trying to move to gain the best shooting position.

In the figures 4-31、4-32, few options are shown.

1) A1 passes to A4 who has run towards the middle line.

2) At the same time A5 creates space in the slot by running towards the rink.

Option 1:

1) When A4 has gained the possession of the ball, he/she passes to A5.

2) At the same time with this pass, A2 moves towards the centre and A3 to the slot.

3) A5 passes to A3 who shoots.

4) A5 can also pass to A2, in which case A3 will screen the goalkeeper when A2 shoots.

3) 边锋以及中锋／前锋应尽力跑动，以获得最佳射门角度。

在图4-31、4-32中有几种选择。

1) A4跑向中线，A1传球给A4；

2) 与此同时，A5沿场边跑动，以创造射门区域及进球空间。

选择一：

1) A4得球后，传给A5；

2) 与此同时，A2向中场跑，A3跑动至射门优势区；

3) A5传球给A3，A3射门；

4) A5也可以传球给A2，这样一来，当A2射门时，A3可以盯防守门员。

Nordic Fashion Sport FLOORBALL

Option 2:

1) A4 passes the ball back to A1 who has moved closer to the rink.

2) A4 covers the middle area by following the pass and A5 assists to defend in case of a turn over.

3) A1 dribbles by the board and passes to A3 who has now moved from the slot towards the rink (creating space in the slot).

4) At the same time with the pass A2 moves to the slot and A5 can also offer a passing opportunity for A3.

5) A3 passes to A2 who shoots.

6) A3 can also pass to A5, in which case A2 will screen the goalkeeper.

7) Players can practice few figures or just use their own

选择二：

1) A1跑动至场边，A4回传球给A1；

2) 传球后A4控制中场区域，A5助攻，以防对手反攻；

3) A1沿板运球，传球给A3，A3此时从射门优势区跑向场边（在优势区创造空位）；

4) 与此同时，A2向射门优势区跑动，A5可以给A3提供传球机会；

5) A3传球给A2，A2射门；

6) A3也可以传球给A5，这样A2便可盯防守门员；

7) 球员可以依照方案进行训练，也可

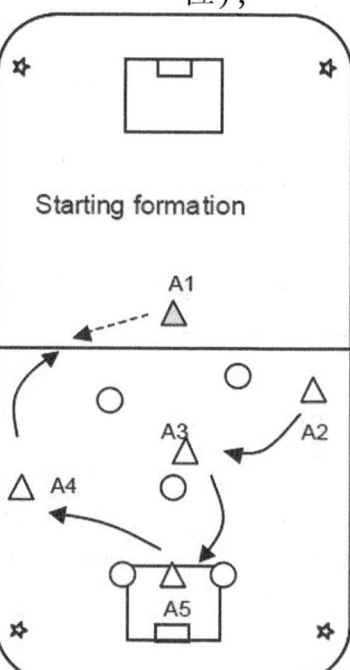

Starting formation

图4-31

第四章 旱地冰球运动的综合技术
Chapter Four　The Basic Technique of Floorball

creativity.

8) First the figures can be practiced without an opponent, and there after adding the opponent playing without sticks and then with sticks.

9) After a shot, there will be another ball in play (passed by the coach or an extra player from the middle line) to begin the drill again.

10) Also defenders can shoot if there is a chance, and then there should always be at least one player screening the goalkeeper.

Modifications:

Variations according to the coaches and players creativity.

Also see drills 11~13.

Key points:

1) Shooting should be emphasized.

2) Players should be ready to shoot (blade on the floor at all times).

以发挥自己的想象力；

8) 首先，可以进行无对手训练，然后加入不持杆对手训练，最后加入持杆对手训练；

9) 射门后，新球加入训练（由教练或非在场球员在中线处传给在场队员），训练重新开始；

10) 有进球机会时，后卫也可以射门，始终应当有至少一名球员盯防守门员。

说明：

可以根据教练及球员创意进行更改。

见常规训练11~13。

训练要点：

1) 重点训练射门；

2) 球员保持随时射门的状态（球板始终着地）；

3)Players should not be afraid to screen the goalkeeper.

4)All the things from previous drills should be brought up and executed during the scrimmage (areas to be avoided on the offensive zone, staying on the shooting sector, screening, creating space for the shot in the slot etc).

5)Use of voice amongst players should be encouraged.

3) 勇于盯防守门员；

4) 交战中，运用之前所有的常规训练(注意规避防守区，射门区，盯防守门员，射门优势区创造射门空间)；

5) 鼓励球员在场上互相言语提醒；

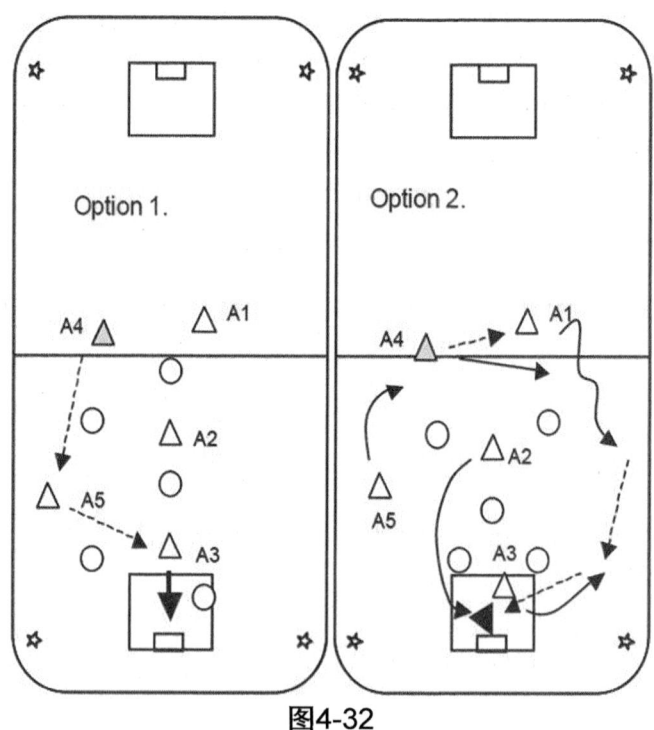

图4-32

第四章　旱地冰球运动的综合技术
Chapter Four　The Basic Technique of Floorball

6)It has to be emphasized that the coach can only provide options, in a game situation it is the player who makes the decisions and those decision have to be suitable for the situation.

7)Also the opponents will have an effect on the play and some options that the coach provides might not be the best ones in certain situations.

6) 应注意教练只是提供训练方案，比赛中是球员做决定，且这些决定必须是适合该特定场合；

7) 同时对手也会影响比赛结果，某种场合下，教练提供的方案并非一定最适合。

3. Dribbling

Level 1

Drill 29

Objective:

To practice ball control and ball handling.

Organization:

Players are standing in front of the coach with one ball each.

Execution:

1) Players dribble the ball standing still keeping head up to see the coach.

2) When the coach shows different signals, the players follow:

①lifting arms up, players move forward,

②pointing arms forward, players move backwards,

③lifting left arm, players move left,

3. 运球

第一阶段

常规训练 29

目的：

练习控球和处理球的能力。

训练安排：

球员每人持球面向教练站好。

训练步骤：

1) 球员站立运球，保持抬头目视教练；

2) 教练给出不同信号，球员遵从：

①教练双臂抬起，球员向前跑动，

②教练双臂前伸，球员后退，

③教练左臂抬起，球员向左跑动，

第四章　旱地冰球运动的综合技术
Chapter Four　The Basic Technique of Floorball

④lifting right arm, players move right,

⑤whistles once, players rotate,

⑥whistles twice, players take a five meters sprint and return to their places.

Modifications:

1) The coach can also come up with numbers to correspond a specific fake, for example: 1 = body fake, 2 = fake using stick.

2) When the coach shouts the number, the players perform the fake.

Key points:

1) Good grip.

2) Game like position.

3) Head up.

④教练右臂抬起，球员向右跑动，

⑤教练吹一次口哨，球员间按顺序循环，

⑥教练吹两次口哨，球员进行5米短距离往返跑。

说明：

1) 教练也可以用特定数字表示假动作，例如：1＝身体假动作，2＝运杆假动作；

2) 教练叫出数字时，球员做出相应假动作。

训练要点：

1) 握杆准确；

2) 赛场站位；

3) 始终抬头。

中国旱地冰球信息网 www.floorballinfo.com
国际旱地冰球联合会 www.floorball.org

Drill 30

Objective:

1) To practice dribbling, fakes, and ball protection.

2) Warm up the players.

Organization and execution:

1) Players run around the rink with one ball each.

2) The coach has set up numbers to correspond a specific action:

①rotation left, continue same direction,

②change of direction with a sprint,

③rotation right, continue same direction,

④lifting the ball up and capturing (continuous movement),

3) Every time the coach shouts the number (or uses whistle) the players perform the move.

常规训练 30

训练目的:

1) 练习运球、假动作及护球;

2) 使队员们热身。

训练组织与步骤:

1) 队员绕场地带球跑;

2) 教练设定号码与具体动作对应:

①向左轮转,方向不变,

②加速变向,

③向右轮转,方向不变,

④向上抛球及接球(连续移动);

3) 每次教练喊号码(或吹哨)球员进行相应动作。

第四章　旱地冰球运动的综合技术
Chapter Four　The Basic Technique of Floorball

Modifications:

   1)Different moves, such as fakes can be added.

   2)Also a shot at both goals to warm up the goalkeepers.

Key points:

   1)Head up.

   2)Game like position.

   3)Other body moves should also be executed during dribbling.

   4)Players should practice stick handling during running.

说明：

   1) 可加上假动作类不同动作；

   2) 两个球门前射门，使守门员热身。

要点：

   1) 抬头；

   2) 赛场位置；

   3) 运球期间可采用其他的身体移动；

   4) 队员跑动中练习使用球杆。

Drill 31

Objective:

To practice ball handling, ball protection, coordination, and both body and ball control.

Organization:

1) Coach sets up the circuit, preferable beforehand or while players are doing the previous exercise.

2) The track should be set up so that there are lot of repetitions and different actions.

3) The whole area should be used efficiently to make the execution intensive and the use of space as economical as possible.

4) Coach explains and demonstrates.

Execution:

1) Players start by bouncing the ball ten times in the air.

2) Forward and backward running.

常规训练 31

训练目的：

练习持球、护球、协调以及控球和身体控制。

训练安排：

1) 教练最好事先或球员做前述练习时划定场域；

2) 设定路线，便于重复和不同动作的反复；

3) 充分利用整个场地加强训练步骤，尽可能节省场地空间；

4) 教练解释并示范。

训练步骤：

1) 队员开始训练空中十次弹球；

2) 前后跑动；

第四章 旱地冰球运动的综合技术
Chapter Four The Basic Technique of Floorball

3)Sideway running, moving the ball from forehand to backhand side.

4)Lifting the ball over an obstacle.

5)Running straight, ball moving around the cones.

6)Stick handling around the cones.

7)Wall passes, running around the cones, ball protection with body.

8)Lifting the ball over an obstacle.

9)Passing the ball between the cones (accuracy) to a goal.

10)starting all over again.

3) 侧跑，正手反手带球；

4) 带球跃过障碍；

5) 直线跑，带球环绕三角锥；

6) 球杆环绕三角锥；

7) 过墙，绕三角锥跑，用身体护球；

8) 带球跃过障碍；

9) 朝球门方向准确传球穿过两个三角锥；

10) 从头开始。

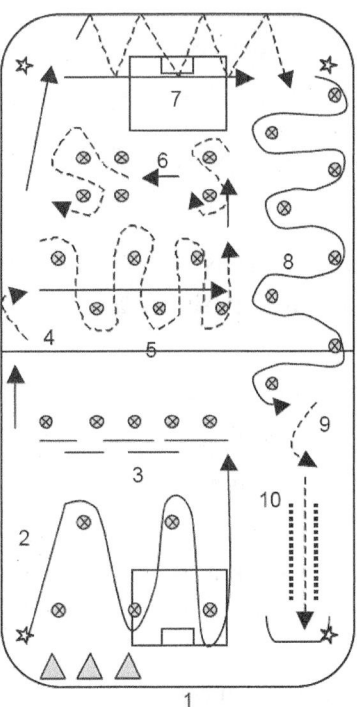

图4-33

Modifications:

1)Different skills can be added, such as shooting and passing.

2)The circuit can be executed without the stick and ball first to practice running and coordination (physical exercise).

Key points:

1)The court should be used efficiently.

2)Players shouldn't be standing on the lines waiting for each turn, in such cases they should be advised to be active with the stick and ball.

3)Also physical exercises can be added, such as abs, push-ups and squats.

4)The circuit can be executed for as long as possible but the coach has to consider the players concentration level.

5)With younger players it is preferable to have less exercises during the circuit so that they won't get confused and forget what is supposed to be done.

说明:

1) 可辅以其他技术，如射门和传球；

2) 可先在无球杆无球的情况下进行跑动和协调性练习（身体素质）。

要点:

1) 充分利用场地；

2) 队员不应在线上等候轮转，这种情况下应该建议队员积极用好球杆和球；

3) 可以增加体能训练，如ABS俯卧撑及下蹲起；

4) 训练尽可能延长，但教练要考虑队员注意力集中程度；

5) 此时年轻队员减少练习，否则他们容易混淆并忘记该做的事。

第四章 旱地冰球运动的综合技术
Chapter Four　The Basic Technique of Floorball

Level 2

Drill 32

Objective:

To practice ball protection and ball handling.

Organization:

Players are divided in pairs.

Execution:

　　1)Players start without sticks with a ball on the floor.

　　2)First one player is protecting the ball by moving around the ball while the other player is trying to kick the ball.

　　3)The ball has to stay still.

　　4)After a minute, the players switch roles.

Modifications:

　　1)To practice ball protection with a stick, the players do the same with sticks using a small area.

　　2)In this case the player with the ball should be using both stick and body to protect the ball.

第二阶段

常规训练 32

训练目的：

　　练习护球和处理球。

训练安排：

　　球员两人一组。

训练步骤：

　　1) 队员开始时不用球杆，将球放在地板上；

　　2) 首先一名队员在球四周移动，以此护球，另一队员试着踢球；

　　3) 球不可被触及；

　　4) 一分钟后角色转换。

说明：

　　1) 球员在狭小空间内用球杆护球，重复上述步骤；

　　2) 此时，有球队员需要同时使用球杆和身体护球；

3)The other player is trying to take the ball away without hitting the stick.

4)When the player without the ball succeeds to take the ball, the roles switch automatically.

5)Also the side of the rink can be used to create a 1 versus 1 situation near the rink or in the corner.

6)In this case the player with the ball should be provided with a solution how to resolve the situation: for example a pass to the sides or behind.

Key points:

1)Low posture (bent knees, legs wide apart).

2)Good grip.

3)No hitting the stick.

4)Continuous movement.

5)Ball handling (the player with the ball has to protect the ball with the blade on the side where the opponent is).

3) 另一球员在避免碰及球杆的情况下夺球；

4) 当无球队员成功得到球时场上角色自动转换；

5) 同时可在边线或底角形成一对一对抗情形；

6) 在此类情况下有球队员需被告知如何处理球：比如向边线或身后传球。

训练要点：

1) 低姿（屈膝双腿分开）；

2) 正确的握杆；

3) 避免触杆；

4) 连续移动；

5) 持球(有球队员需要以面向对手的击球板护球)。

第四章 旱地冰球运动的综合技术
Chapter Four　The Basic Technique of Floorball

Drill 33

Objective:

1) To practice ball protection and ball handling.

2) To practice fakes.

3) To practice decision making in two against two situations.

4) To develop the player's ability to hold possession of the ball in a tight situation.

Organization:

1) Players are divided in pairs.

2) The rink is divided in quarters.

3) Two couples in each quarter.

Execution:

1) Players start playing two against two game when the coach whistles.

2) The ball carrier has to make a fake before passing to a team mate.

常规训练 33

训练目的：

1) 练习护球及持球；

2) 练习假动作；

3) 练习在二对二的情况下处理球的决断能力；

4) 练习在紧逼情况下守住球的能力。

训练安排：

1) 队员两两一组；

2) 球场分为四部分；

3) 每四分之一球场两对球员。

训练步骤：

1) 教练鸣哨时队员进行二对二的对抗练习；

2) 持球队员传球给队友前需做一次假动作；

3)When the opponent manages to steal the ball, the roles switch automatically.

4)Game is played until the coach whistles.

5)The length of the shift can be varied from 45 seconds to 2 minutes where after there can be a short recovery break or the players can switch the opponent.

Modifications:

1)Also other rules can be implemented such as, the couple with the ball has to cross and make a drop pass before passing.

2)The drill can also be played using the corner area, with goals facing the boards so a shot can be added.

3)This will emphasize play

3)对手抢断成功后,场上角色自动转换;

4)教练再次鸣哨后方可结束;

5)每回合持续时间45秒至2分钟不等,之后可有短暂调整休息时间,队员可互换角色。

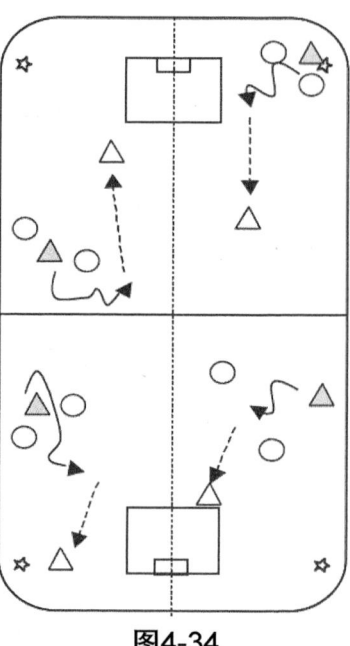

图4-34

说明:

1)可另加规则,如持球二人需在吊球传球前交叉跑动;

2)此类训练可以在底角区域进行,球门面向档球板,可加入射门练习;

3)此训练强调在较小区

第四章 旱地冰球运动的综合技术
Chapter Four The Basic Technique of Floorball

in a small area and gain a scoring chance in a tight situation.

Key points:

1)Head up (awareness of both the team mate and the opponents).

2)The ball carrier has to make a fake before passing.

3)The ball carrier has to protect the ball and dribble until he/she is ready to make a fake.

4)Players should be encouraged to challenge the opponent.

5)Both defending players should try to double the ball carrier and the other offensive player should create a passing lane by getting close to the ball carrier.

6)The other offensive player can also create space for the ball carrier by screening the opponent.

域紧逼情况下得分。

训练要点:

1)抬头(关注队友和对手);

2) 传球前持球队员必须做假动作;

3) 持球队员在准备做假动作前必须护球并运球;

4) 鼓励队员对抗对手;

5) 两名防守队员需尽力包夹持球队员,而另一进攻球员需尽可能靠近持球队员以创造出传球路线;

6) 另一进攻队员可以干扰对手为持球队员创造空间。

·167·

Nordic Fashion Sport FLOORBALL

Drill 34

Objective:

1) To practice ball protection and ball handling.

2) To practice decision making as a ball carrier.

Organization:

1) Players are divided in groups of three (or four with a substitute player).

2) Rink divided in half, with two goals on each side.

3) Goal cages can be replaced by cones.

Execution:

1) Three against three game.

2) Players are only allowed to pass backwards.

3) Therefore they have to dribble the ball forward to pass.

4) The ball also has to be passed to each player once before scoring.

5) Every time the opponent scores, the team who didn't

常规训练 34

训练目的：

1) 练习护球及持球；

2) 练习持球者在处理球时候的决断能力。

训练安排：

1) 球员分为每三人一组（或者四人一组，包括替补队员）；

2) 球场分为两个半场，每边各有一球门；

3) 球门可由锥筒代替。

训练步骤：

1) 三对三对抗练习；

2) 球员只能向后传球；

3) 因此球员必须向前运球以传球；

4) 得分前球必须经过所有球员之手一次；

5) 每次对手得分之后，

第四章　旱地冰球运动的综合技术
Chapter Four　The Basic Technique of Floorball

score have to do push-ups or sit-ups which can also be executed after one shift.

失分队做俯卧撑或仰卧起坐，也可以一个回合之后再做。

Modifications:

1)Also man coverage emphasizes the technical ability to protect the ball.

2)The game can also be played with one goal using half of the rink as in drill 27.

Key points:

1)Players should be aware of where the opponent as well as the team mates are situated.

2)Non-ball carriers should create passing lanes behind the ball carrier as he/she is allowed to only pass backwards.

3)The rules should be strictly followed and equal.

说明：

1) 盯防强调战术上的护球能力；

2) 这个训练也可以用一个球门半场进行，如常规训练27。

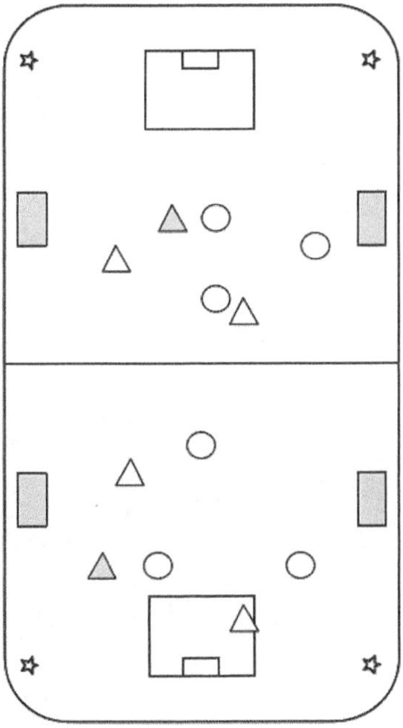

图4-35

训练要点：

1) 队员要清楚对手和队友所在位置；

2) 因持球队员仅能向后传球，无球队员要在其身后创造传球路线；

3) 严格遵守规则，公平公正。

·169·

北欧时尚运动——旱地冰球
Nordic Fashion Sport FLOORBALL

Section Two: The Comprehension of Match Tactics

Tactics is the attacking and defending strategies adopting in the game to defeat the opposing team, which includes:

1)Attacking tactics, including single, 2-3 team members and team attacking tactics. The whole team tactics consists of fast attack and positional attack.

2)Defending tactics, including single, 2-3 players and team defending tactics.

第二节　比赛战术认识

战术是比赛中为了战胜对方而采取的攻防方法。它包括：

1) 进攻战术，有个人、2~3人和全队的进攻战术，全队进攻战术又可分为快攻和阵地进攻；

2) 防守战术，分为个人防守、2~3人防守和全队防守战术；

第四章 旱地冰球运动的综合技术
Chapter Four The Basic Technique of Floorball

3) "Power play" and "few to defeat many" tactics. There is a rule of 2 and 5 minutes suspension, so it might appear a situation of "power play" on the field, for example "6 vs. 5 or 4". The "power play" tactics is the special attacking tactics aiming at this situation, which is the best moment to score. Whereas "few to defeat many" is the special defending tactics forced to use when suspension occurs.

3)"以多打少"和"以少打多"战术,旱地冰球规则有罚出场2分钟和5分钟的规定,场上可能形成6打5或6打4的"以多打少"局面,这是得分的最好时机,"以多打少"战术就是针对这一情况采取的一种特殊形式的进攻战术;反之少打多则是因队员被罚出场而被迫采取的特殊形式的防守战术。

第五章　旱地冰球重大赛事
Chapter Five　Important Floorball Events

World Championships (men and women).

U19 World Championships (men and women).

Euro Floorball Cup(men and women).

Champions Cup and EFC every year.

International tournaments 3-5 per year.

International matches(100 matches).

IFF Sanctioned international tournaments: e.g... Austrian Open, Czech Open, Lushnik Open (Moscow).

世界冠军联赛（男子和女子）；

19岁以下青年冠军联赛（男子和女子）；

欧洲杯（男子和女子）；

冠军杯和欧洲杯（每年举行一次）；

国际锦标赛（每年举行3-5届）；

国际性的比赛（约100场）；

国际旱地冰球联合会认可的国际锦标赛：例如澳大利亚公开赛、捷克公开赛以及莫斯科公开赛。

第五章　旱地冰球综合知识
Chapter Five　The Basic Knowledge of Floorball

1. World Floorball Championships men

WFC for men every even year

    2002　in Finland

    2004　in Switzerland

    2006　in Sweden

    2008　in Czech Republic

    2010　in Finland

    2012　in Switzerland

WFC Finals, 16 teams

    Reigning World Champions from 2010: Finland

    Silver: Sweden

    Bronze: Switzerland

    The World Championships since 2002 have been broadcasted by the respective national broadcasting companies.

    The finals of the WFC since 2004 has been broadcasted live on Eurosport.

1. 世界男子旱地冰球冠军联赛

每偶数年举办一次世界男子旱地冰球冠军联赛

2002年 芬兰

2004年 瑞士

2006年 瑞典

2008年 捷克共和国

2010年 芬兰

2012年 瑞士

世界旱地冰球冠军联赛决赛球队有16支

2010年世界旱地冰球冠军联赛冠军：芬兰

亚军：瑞典

季军：瑞士

自2002年起，世界冠军联赛赛事就已被各国的广播公司进行转播。

自2004年起，世界冠军联赛就已在欧洲范围内进行现场直播。

北欧时尚运动——旱地冰球
Nordic Fashion Sport FLOORBALL

2. World Floorball Championships women

2.世界女子旱地冰球冠军联赛

WFC for women every odd year

每奇数年举办世界女子旱地冰球冠军联赛

    2003 in Switzerland

    2005 in Singapore

    2007 in Denmark

    2009 in Sweden

    2011 in Switzerland

2003年 瑞士

2005年 新加坡

2007年 丹麦

2009年 瑞典

2011年 瑞士

    WFC Finals, 16 teams

世界旱地冰球冠军联赛决赛球队有16支

    Reigning World Champions from 2009: Sweden

2009年世界旱地冰球冠军联赛冠军：瑞典

第五章 旱地冰球综合知识
Chapter Five The Basic Knowledge of Floorball

Silver: Switzerland	亚军：瑞士
Bronze: Finland	季军：芬兰

3. World Floorball Championships U19
3. 世界旱地冰球19岁以下青年冠军联赛

1) WFC U19 for men every odd year

1) 男子世界旱地冰球19岁以下青年冠军联赛每奇数年举办

16 nations participating

共有来自16个国家的球队参赛

2001 in Germany	2001年 德国
2003 in Czech Republic	2003年 捷克共和国
2005 in Latvia	2005年 拉脱维亚
2007 in Switzerland	2007年 瑞士
2009 in Finland	2009年 芬兰
2011 in Germany	2011年 德国

Reigning World Champions from 2011: Finland

2011年世界19岁以下青年冠军联赛冠军：芬兰

2) WFC U19 for women every even year

2) 女子世界旱地冰球19岁以下青年冠军联赛每偶数年举办

2004: in Finland first time	2004年 首次在芬兰举办
2006: in Germany	2006年 德国
2008: in Poland	2008年 波兰

北欧时尚运动——旱地冰球
Nordic Fashion Sport FLOORBALL

2010: in Czech Republic

Reigning World Champion from 2010: Sweden

4.Euro Floorball Cup

The Euro Floorball Cup for national club team champions every year for both men and women.

EFC Finals for 8 best club teams men and women:

2004 in Germany
2005 in Switzerland
2006 in Czech Republic
2007 in Sweden

2010年 捷克共和国

2010年世界U19冠军联赛冠军：瑞典

4.旱地冰球欧洲杯

每年，在各国的俱乐部球队间举办男子及女子欧洲杯冠军赛。

旱地冰球欧洲杯决赛会在8支最优秀的俱乐部球队间展开：

2004年 德国
2005年 瑞士
2006年 捷克共和国
2007年 瑞典

第五章 旱地冰球综合知识
Chapter Five The Basic Knowledge of Floorball

2008 in Finland	2008年 芬兰
2009 in Switzerland	2009年 瑞士
2009 in Denmark	2009年 丹麦
2010 in Latvia	2010年 拉脱维亚

Reigning EFC Champions men from 2010: Storvreta, Sweden.

2010年旱地冰球欧洲杯男子冠军队是：瑞典的斯托莱塔

Reigning EFC Champions for women 2010: IKSU, Sweden

2010年旱地冰球欧洲杯女子冠军队是：瑞典的IKSU

第六章 旱地冰球竞赛规则
Chapter Six The Rules for Game

(International Floorball Federation——Rules and Competition Committee)

（国际旱地冰球协会——规则与竞赛委员会）

Conditions of the Game

Floorball shall be played in the form of a match between two teams. The aim of the game is to score more goals than the opposing team, whilst playing within the limits of the rules.

　　Preferably, floorball shall be played indoors on a hard and even surface at a venue that has been approved by the administrating authority.

比赛形式

　　旱地冰球比赛应在两支球队之间进行，在规则允许范围内，以获得比对方更多进球为目的。

　　建议比赛在经过认证的室内平坦坚硬的球场举行。

第六章　旱地冰球竞赛规则
Chapter Six　The Rules for Game

Section One: Rink

101 Dimensions of the rink

1) The rink shall be 40m×20 m and enclosed by a board with rounded corners, which is approved by the IFF and marked accordingly.

2) The rink shall be rectangular, the measures indicating length x width. The smallest rink allowed is 36 m×18 m, and the largest is 44 m×22 m.

102 Markings on the rink

1) All markings shall be made with lines, 4-5 cm in width, in a clearly visible color.

2) A centre line and a centre spot shall be marked. The centre line shall be parallel to the short sides of the rink and divide the rink into two halves of equal size.

第一节　比赛场地

101　比赛场地的尺寸

1) 场地规格为40米长，20米宽，周边有挡板，挡板四角为圆角，经IFF认证并有相应标记。

2) 场地为长方形，测量标准为长乘宽，获准最小尺寸长36米、宽18米，最大尺寸长44米，宽22米。

102　场地标记

1) 所有的标记为线型，宽4-5cm，颜色清晰可辨。

2) 必须标明中线和中心点；中线应与短边平行，并将场地平分为两份。

3)Goal creases measuring 4 m x 5 m shall be marked 2.85 m from the short sides of the rink. The goal creases shall be centred in relation to the long sides of the rink.

4)Goalkeeper areas measuring 1 m × 2.5 m shall be marked 0.65 m in front of the rear limits of the goal creases.

The goalkeeper areas shall be rectangular, and the measures indicate length × width including the lines. The goalkeeper areas shall be centred in relation to the long sides of the rink.

5)The rear lines of the goalkeeper areas shall also serve as goal lines. Marks for the goal posts shall be made on the rear lines of the goalkeeper areas, so that the distance between the marks is 1.6 m.

The goal lines shall be centred in relation to the long sides of the rink. The marks for the goal posts shall be made

3) 球门禁区5米长，4米宽，距球场短边2.85米，测量尺寸含线宽。球门区相对场地长边居中。

4)守门员区域大小为1米宽，2.5米长，在球门禁区前方0.65米处。

该区域为长方形，长、宽测量含线的宽度，相对球场的两个长边居中。

5) 球门禁区底线即为进球有效线，球门柱标示点在球门区底线，标示点相距1.6米。

球门线相对球场长边居中，球门柱标示可以切断球门区底线或画一条与球门线

第六章 旱地冰球竞赛规则
Chapter Six The Rules for Game

either with interruptions in the rear lines of the goalkeeper area or with short line, perpendicular to the rear lines of the goalkeeper area.

6)Face-off dots shall be marked on the centre line and on the imaginary extensions of the goal lines, 1.5 m from the long sides of the rink not exceeding 30 cm in diameter.

The face-off dots shall be marked as crosses. The dots on the centre line may be imaginary.

103 Goal cages

1)Goal cages, approved by the IFF and marked accordingly, shall be placed with the posts on the prescribed marks.

2)The openings of the goal cages shall face the centre spot.

垂直的短线作为球门放置的标志。

6) 争球点，应当标明在中线和球门线的虚拟延长线上，距离场地长边1.5米，直径不超过30cm。

争球点应用十字交叉线标明，中线上的开球点可以不予标明。

103 球门

1) IFF认证和专门标识的球门置于事先标示处。

2) 球门开口朝向场地中心。

104 Substitution zones

1) Substitution zones with a length of 10 m shall be marked along one of the long sides of the rink, 5 m from the centre line, and include players' benches.

2) The substitution zones shall be marked on both sides of the board. The width of the substitution zones shall not exceed 3 m, measured from the board. The players' benches shall be placed at an appropriate distance from the board and have room for nineteen persons each.

3) The substitution zone can also be marked on top of the rink, using a different color.

105 Secretariat and penalty benches

1) A secretariat with penalty benches shall be placed opposite the substitution zones, by the centre line.

2) The secretariat and the penalty benches shall be placed at an appropriate distance from the board.

104 休息区

1）休息区长10米，与球场长边平行，距离中线5米，备有运动员休息长凳。

2）挡板两侧各有休息区标记，休息区宽度距挡板不超3米，板凳可容纳19人，离挡板有一定距离。

3）也可以在球场顶端用不同颜色标示休息区。

105 记录员席及处罚席

1）场地另外一侧正对休息区处的中线附近设记录员席及处罚席，记录员席及处罚席与挡板距离适中。

2）记录席两边为两队分设处罚席，每个可容两人位置。

3) There shall be separate penalty benches for each team, placed on each side of the secretariat. The penalty benches shall have room for at least two persons each. Exemption for the placing of the secretariat and the penalty benches may be given by the administrating authority. If this is the case there shall be left a minimum of 2 m space in between the penalty bench and the substitution benches.

106 Inspection of the rink

1) The referees shall, at an early stage before the match, inspect the rink and ensure that defects are corrected.

2) All defects shall be reported. The organiser is responsible for correcting defects and for keeping the board in a proper condition during the match. All dangerous objects shall be removed or padded.

3) 官方每一支队伍都应配备处罚席，放置于每队的记录员席内，处罚席需可容纳两个人。官方有权摆放两队的记录员席和处罚席，处罚席需至少与替补席隔开两米的距离。

106 场地的检验

1) 比赛开始前，裁判员检查场地，督促主办方修正不合格处。

2) 所有不合格处均要报告，主办方负责修正并确保比赛过程中挡板处于适合状态，一切危险物品均应移除或加衬垫。

Section Two: The Game

201 Regular game time

1) Regular game time shall be 3×20 minutes with two 10 minute intermissions, when the teams shall change ends.

①Exemption for shorter game time however not less than 2×15 minutes and/or intermissions may be given by the administrating authority.

②When changing ends, the teams shall also change substitution zones.

③The home team shall choose ends at an early stage before the match.

④Every new period shall start with a face-off at the centre spot.

⑤At the end of every period the secretariat is responsible for providing a siren or other suitable sound device, unless this is automatic.

第二节 比赛时间

201 常规比赛时间

1) 正规比赛时间应当为3节，每节20分钟，节间休息10分钟，且两队交换场地。

①比赛时间最多可缩至两节，每节15分钟，中场休息由主管领导决定；

②球队交换场地的同时，也应交换休息区；

③主场队有权在赛前优先挑选场地；

④每节开始时，应在中点面对面争球；

⑤每节比赛结束时，若没有自动报时，则记录员需鸣哨或使用其他合适的高音设施提醒时间已到；

第六章 旱地冰球竞赛规则
Chapter Six The Rules for Game

⑥The timing of the intermission shall start immediately at the end of the period.

⑦The teams are responsible for being back onto the rink in time to resume play after the intermission.

⑧If the referees consider one end of the rink to be better, the teams shall change ends after half the third period, but this has to be decided before the start of the third period. If such a changing of ends takes place, play shall be resumed with a face-off at the centre spot.

2)Game time shall be effective.

①Effective game time implies that time shall be stopped whenever play is interrupted by the referees' whistle, and started again when the ball is played.

②At unnatural game interruptions a triple signal shall be used. The referees decide what shall be regarded as an unnatural interruption, but this always

⑥每节比赛一结束，休息时间立即开始计时；

⑦球队应及时返回场地以开始下一节的比赛；

⑧如果裁判认为场地的某一侧更好，则参赛队应在第三节进行到一半时交换场地（必须在第三节开始之前决定）。交换场地后应从中线争球开始继续比赛。

2) 比赛时间确保有效。

①裁判鸣哨，无论状况如何，比赛停止，一旦开球，开始计时；

②三声哨响即非常规中断比赛，包括：球的损坏，挡板散开，有人受伤，设备检查，无关人员或物体进入

·185·

includes: a damaged ball, the board coming apart, injuries, measuring of equipment, unauthorised persons or objects on the rink, the lights going out either completely or partly, and the final signal being sounded by mistake.

③Should the board come apart play shall not be interrupted until the ball is near the place in question.

④In case of injuries play shall be interrupted only on suspicion of a serious injury or if the injured player directly affects play.

⑤An administrating authority may grant an exemption to use non-effective time, in which case game time shall only be stopped in connection with a goal, a penalty, a penalty shot, a time out or at the referees' triple signal at an unnatural interruption. The last 3 minutes of regular game time shall always be effective.

⑥Game time shall be stopped during a penalty shot.

场地，灯完全或部分失明，误吹结束哨等；

③挡板散落时可以继续比赛，除非球在该挡板附近且影响了比赛动作；

④只在严重受伤或者该受伤队员影响比赛时需中断比赛；

⑤主管方允许部分非比赛时间处理以下情况，如进球，判罚，罚球，暂停，或因为裁判三声哨响示意的比赛中断，但常规时间的最后3分钟务必连续有效；

⑥罚球时应停止计时。

第六章　旱地冰球竞赛规则
Chapter Six　The Rules for Game

202 Time out

During the match each team shall have the right to request time out, and be marked by a triple signal as soon as play is interrupted.

A time out may be requested at any time, including in connection with goals and penalty shots, penalty shots after limited extra time excluded, but only by the team captain or a member of the team staff.

A time out requested during an interruption shall be carried out immediately, but if the referees consider that this negatively affects the situation for the opposing team, the time out shall be carried out at the next interruption. A requested time out shall always be carried out, except after a goal, when the team may withdraw the request.

A time out starts at the referees' additional signal when the teams are at their substitution zones and the referees at the

202 暂停

整场比赛中每队都有一次要求暂停的权利，此时裁判应鸣哨三声示意比赛中断。

暂停可以在任何时间进行，包括进球和罚球时，也包括加时赛后的点球战，但暂停的要求只能由球队的队长或队员提出。

比赛中断时，暂停要求应当立刻得到许可，但如果裁判认为此时局面对另一方不利则暂停可在下一次中断时执行。暂停要求一般会被许可，除非进球后主动撤回请求。

裁判加哨提示后球员到休息区，裁判到计分区，暂停计时开始，30秒后的另一声哨响暂停结束。

secretariat. Another additional signal after 30 seconds marks the end of the time out.

After a time out, play shall be resumed according to what caused the interruption. A penalized player is not allowed to participate in a time out.

203 Extra time

If a match that has to be decided ends with an even result 10 minutes extra time shall be played until one team scores.

Before extra time, the teams have the right to a 2 minutes intermission, but no changing of ends shall take place. During extra time the same rules apply to starting and stopping time as during regular game time. Extra time is not divided into periods. Penalty time remaining after regular game time shall continue during extra time. If the score after limited extra time is still equal, the match shall be decided by penalty shots.

暂停后，比赛应从引起比赛中断的局面开始继续，受罚队员不得参与暂停。

203 加时赛

如果比赛平局，则可以进行10分钟的加时赛直到有一队得分为止。

加时赛开始前休息2分钟，但不进行场地交换。在加时赛中规则与常规时间完全一致，加时赛不分节，常规时间中剩余的处罚时间应连续计时，如果比分在加时赛后仍持平，则进行点球决战。

第六章　旱地冰球竞赛规则
Chapter Six　The Rules for Game

204 Penalty shots after extra time

1)Five field players from each team shall take one penalty shot each. If the score after this is still equal, the same players shall take one penalty shot each until a decisive result is achieved.

The penalty shots shall be taken alternately. The referees decide which goal to use and shall carry out a draw between the team captains. The winner decides which team will start taking the penalty shots. The team captain or a member of the team staff shall, in writing, inform the referees and the secretariat of the numbers of the players and the order in which they will take the penalty shots. The referees are responsible for ensuring that the penalty shots are taken in the exact order as noted by the team staff.

2)As soon as a decisive result is achieved during the penalty shots, the match is over

204 加时赛后点球决战

1) 两队各五名在场球员每人进行罚点球，如此后比分依然相同，则按原来点球次序继续直至分出胜负。

点球两队依次进行，裁判员决定使用某一侧球门，两队队长抽签挑边，胜者有权选择哪一队先开始罚球，队长或队中的某一队员必须手写通知裁判和记录席该队罚点球的队员号码及次序，裁判确保该组队员按字条顺序依次进行罚球。

2) 一旦罚点球决出胜负，则比赛立即结束，胜队视同因一个额外进球而获胜。

·189·

and the winning team shall be considered to have won by one extra goal.

During the regular penalty shots, a decisive result is considered to be achieved when a team is leading by a larger number of goals than the opposing team has remaining penalty shots. During the possible extra penalty shots, a decisive result is considered to be achieved when a team has scored one goal more than the opposing team and both teams have taken the same number of penalty shots. The extra penalty shots do not have to be taken in the same order as the regular penalty shots, but a player must not take his third penalty shot until all the noted players in his team have taken at least two, and so on.

3) A penalized player may participate in the penalty shots if he has not incurred a match penalty.

在点球战中，当一队以大比分领先对方剩余罚球次数时，则点球战提前结束。同时当两队进行了相同的罚球次数时，某队领先一球即为胜队，在延长的点球战中，队员无需按照常规点球战的次序进行主罚，但在所有队员都完成至少两次罚球之前，不得有队员进行第三次罚球。

3) 没有受到停赛处罚的受罚队员也可以参与点球战。

第六章　旱地冰球竞赛规则
Chapter Six　　The Rules for Game

If one of the noted players incurs any penalty during the penalty shots, the team captain shall choose a field player, who is not already noted, to replace the player who has incurred the penalty. If a goalkeeper incurs any penalty during the penalty shots, he shall be replaced by the reserve goalkeeper. If a reserve goalkeeper is not available, the team has a maximum of 3 minutes to properly equip a field player, who is not already noted, but none of this time may be used for warming up. The new goalkeeper shall be marked in the match record, and the time of the change shall be noted.

4)A team that is unable to note five field players shall only be allowed to take as many penalty shots as they have noted players. This is also valid during possible extra penalty shots.

如果点球战的队员在罚球中违规受到处罚，则队长可以选择一名新的场员进行替补。如果点球战中守门员受处罚，则必须更换守门员，如果没有替补守门员，则该队最多有3分钟选择一名替补队员出任守门员，但不允许有热身时间。比赛记录纸上标明新的守门员，同时记录替补的时间。

4) 如果某队无法提供五名队员参与罚球，则只能进行与球员数目相同的罚球，同样在罚球战的延长期中也应当依照此例。

Section Three: Participants

301 Players

1) Each team is allowed to use a maximum of 20 players. These shall be noted in the match record.

Players may be field players or goalkeepers. No other players than those noted in the match record are allowed to participate in the match or be in their own substitution zones.

2) During play at the most six players in each team, including only one goalkeeper or six field players only, may be on the rink simultaneously.

For the referees to start a match, each team shall have at least five field players and a properly equipped goalkeeper, or the final score shall be 5-0 to the nonoffending team. During play, each team must be able to play with at least four players, or

第三节 参赛人员

301 队员

1) 每队最多可报名20名队员，且均应在比赛记录纸上登记。

队员含场员或守门员，未在记录纸上登录的队员不得进入休息区。

2) 比赛过程中每队最多使用六名队员，其中包括一名守门员，或者比赛中只有六名场员同时上场。

裁判确定比赛开始时，每队都应至少有5名场员和1名正确穿着护具的守门员，否则比赛将以5∶0结束，非违规队获胜。且每个队至少有四名球员在场进行比赛，否则比赛将以5-0结束，非

第六章　旱地冰球竞赛规则
Chapter Six　The Rules for Game

the match shall be stopped and the final score shall be 5-0 to the non-offending team.

违规队获胜。

302 Substitution of players

302 队员的替换

Substitution of players may take place at any time and an unlimited number of times during a match.

比赛中替换队员不限次数，且随时可换。

All substitution shall take place in the team's own substitution zone. A player leaving the rink has to be on his way passing over the board before a substitute may enter the rink.

所有换人都应发生在球队的休息区。必须在被替换球员出挡板之后，替换的球员才能入场。

An injured player leaving the rink outside his own substitution zone must not be replaced until play is interrupted.

本队休息区域外离场的受伤队员比赛中断之前，不得被替换。

303 Particular regulations for goalkeepers

303 守门员的特殊规定

1) All goalkeepers shall be marked in the match record.

1) 所有的守门员均应在在比赛记录中标明。

The marking shall be made with a "G" in the margin. A player marked as goalkeeper is

守门员以字母"G"在页边的空白处标记，守门员

• 193 •

not allowed to participate as a field player, with a stick, during the same match. If a team due to injury or penalty has to replace the goalkeeper with a field player, they have a maximum of 3 minutes to properly equip the substitute, but none of this time shall be used for warming up. The new goalkeeper shall be marked in the match record, and the time of the change shall be noted.

2)If a goalkeeper entirely leaves his goal crease during play, he shall, until he returns, be considered a field player, yet without a stick.

This does not apply in connection with a throw-out. A goalkeeper is considered to have entirely left the goal crease when no part of his body touches the floor inside the goal crease. The goalkeeper is, however, allowed to jump within his own goal crease. The lines belong to the goal crease.

不得作为持杆的场员上场。在比赛中，如果守门员因受伤或者处罚而必须用场员更换守门员时，最多有3分钟时间来整理装备，但没有时间用于热身，在比赛记录纸上标明新的守门员，同时记录替补的时间。

2) 如果守门员完全离开球门区，则他在回到球门区之前应被认为是一名无球杆的场员。

守门员离开球门区，不允许用手进行传接球。所谓完全离开球门区，是指没有任何身体部分接触球门区地面，但允许守门员在球门区起跳接球，球门线为球门区一部分。

第六章　旱地冰球竞赛规则

Chapter Six　The Rules for Game

304 Particular regulations for team captains

1)Each team shall have a team captain, who shall be marked in the match record. The marking shall be made with a "C" in the margin.

Change of the team captain shall only take place in case of injury, illness or match penalty, and has to be noted with time in the match record. A replaced team captain must not function again as team captain during the same match.

2)Only the team captain is entitled to speak to the referees. He is also obliged to assist them.

When the team captain speaks to the referees, this shall be done according to set conditions.

A penalized team captain loses his right to speak to the referees, unless he is addressed by them, and, except when the team staff requests a time out, the team has no possibility to communicate with the referees.

304 队长的特殊规则

1)每队都应有一名队长,且以字母"C"在比赛记录上标明。

只有在受伤、生病、比赛处罚的情况下才可以更换队长,同时应在记录纸上注明更换以及相应时间。被替换的队长在比赛中不得重新成为队长。

2)只有队长有权与裁判进行对话,同时有义务协助裁判。

队长只能在条件与规则允许的范围内与裁判交换意见。

受罚队长无权与裁判对话,裁判要求对话时除外,或当球队队员拟请求暂停,但无法与裁判进行交流时除外。

If considered necessary by the referee discussions shall be taken in the corridors and not in the rink and never inside the referees' dressing room.

305 Team staff

Each team shall note at the most five members of the team staff in the match record.

No other persons than those noted in the match record are allowed to be in their own substitution zone. With the exception of a time out, a member of the team staff shall not enter the rink without the referees' permission. All coaching shall take place from the team's own substitution zone. Before the match, a member of the team staff shall sign the match record. After the start of the match no amendments shall be allowed except from possible corrections of incorrect numbering. Should a member of the team staff be recorded also as a player, he should always be considered a

如裁判认为有必要，可以在走廊内讨论，但不能在场地讨论也不能在裁判休息室中进行。

305 球队工作人员

每队最多可以申报5名球队工作人员，除此以外的其他人员不得进入休息区。

除暂停外，未经裁判允许球队工作人员不得进入比赛场地，所有指导都应在球队休息区进行。比赛开始前，球队工作人员应当在记录纸上签字，比赛开始后，除更正错误号码外不得做其他任何更改。如果工作人员同时被报名为球队队员，鉴于休息区规则，任何不确定状况下，他都将被认定是一名队员。

Chapter Six The Rules for Game
第六章 旱地冰球竞赛规则

player in any uncertain situations regarding offences in the substitution zone.

306 Referees

A match shall be led and controlled by two equally authorized referees.

The referees shall have the right to stop a match if there is an obvious risk that it cannot be continued according to the rules.

307 Secretariat

A secretariat shall be in place.

The secretariat shall be neutral and responsible for the match record, time keeping and possible speaker tasks.

306 裁判员

一场比赛应有两名同等认证的裁判员掌控。

裁判有权根据规则，在发现有明显危及比赛进行的情况下中止比赛。

307 记录员

记录员应位于记录席，客观、负责地记录比赛情况，提醒时间，可能情况下担任广播员。

中国旱地冰球信息网 www.floorballinfo.com
国际旱地冰球联合会 www.floorball.org

Section Four: Equipment

401 The players' clothing

1) All field players shall wear uniforms consisting of jerseys, shorts and knee socks.

All field players in a team shall wear the exact same uniform. Women may wear short skirts or dresses (shirt and skirt in one piece) instead of shorts. A team's uniform may have any color combination, but the jerseys must not be grey. If the referees consider that the teams cannot be distinguished by their uniforms, the visiting team is obliged to change. The socks shall be pulled up to the knees, mutually uniform and, if decided by the administrating authority, distinguishable between the teams.

2) All goalkeepers shall be dressed in jerseys and long trousers.

第四节　装备

401 队员的服装

1) 所有运动员统一着装，含球衣、短裤和长膝袜。

球队所有在场队员穿完全相同的比赛服，女性可以穿短裙或连衣裙（衬衫和短裙一体）代替短裤。比赛服可以多色一体，但球衣不可为灰色，如果裁判认为两队球衣难以区分，则客队应更换比赛服。长袜应该过膝，且与队服颜色统一，如果由管理层决定，两队着装务必有明显差别。

2) 所有守门员须穿球衣和长裤。

第六章　旱地冰球竞赛规则
Chapter Six　The Rules for Game

3)All jerseys shall be numbered.

A team's jerseys shall be numbered with different whole numbers in clearly visible Arabic figures on the back and on the chest. The back figures shall be at least 200 mm high and the chest figures at least 70 mm high. The jerseys may carry any number between 1 and 99 inclusive, but 1 is not allowed for field players. If an incorrectly numbered player participates in the match, the match record shall be corrected and the offence shall be reported to the administrating authority.

4)All players shall wear shoes.

The shoes shall be of an indoor sports model. Socks outside the shoes are not allowed. If a player loses one or both shoes during play, he may continue playing until the next interruption.

3) 所有球衣应有背号。

球衣背号为不同的整数阿拉伯数字且清晰标于球衣的前胸和后背，后背的背号应当至少20cm高，胸部的号码至少7cm高，球衣号码可以介于1和99之间，但1号不能是场上运动员的号码。如果在场比赛队员号码有误，记录员应进行订正并将违规情况报告主管部门。

4) 所有球员必须穿球鞋。

球鞋应当适应室内运动，袜子不得穿在球鞋的外面，如果在比赛中，队员的球鞋脱落，他可以继续参加比赛直至下一次比赛中断。

402 The referees' clothing

The referees shall wear jerseys, black shorts and black knee socks.

The referees shall wear the same color combination on their uniform.

403 Particular goalkeeper's equipment

1) The goalkeeper is not allowed to use a stick.

2) The goalkeeper shall wear a face mask, which is in accordance with the IFF Material Regulations and marked accordingly.

This only includes on the rink during play. All tampering with the face mask, except painting, is prohibited.

3) The goalkeeper may use any kind of protective equipment, but this shall not include parts intended to cover the goal.

402 裁判员的服装

裁判应该穿裁判服，黑短裤和黑色过膝袜。

裁判服应保持色彩一致。

403 守门员的特殊装备

1) 守门员不允许使用球杆。

2) 守门员可以带经IFF认可的面具，且只可在场内比赛进行中使用。禁止对面具进行改造（换颜色除外）。

3) 守门员可以使用保护装备，但不含增加防守面积遮挡球门的情况。

第六章　旱地冰球竞赛规则

Chapter Six　　The Rules for Game

4)Helmet and thin gloves are allowed. All forms of adhesives or friction checking substances are prohibited. No objects must be kept on or in the goal cage. The goalkeeper may not use any kind of protective equipment which covers more than the body of the goalkeeper, for example shoulder pads.

404　Particular team captain's equipment

The team captain shall wear an armlet.

　　The armlet shall be worn on the arm and be clearly visible. Tape is not allowed as an armlet. Incorrect armlet shall be reported to the administrating authority.

405　Personal equipment

A player shall not wear personal equipment which may cause injury.

　　Personal equipment includes protective and medical equipment, watches, earrings, etc.

4) 守门员可以戴头盔和薄手套，禁止使用各种形式的粘合剂以及提高摩擦力的物品；不得在球门内或上方放置任何物品，同时不允许守门员使用任何覆盖面积超过其身体的护具，如垫肩等。

404　队长的特殊装备

队长必须戴袖标。

袖标应清晰可见，但禁止使用胶带，不合法的袖标应报主管方审定。

405　个人装备

球员不得穿着可能造成伤害的装备。

个人装备包括带有防护效果或者医疗效果的设备，如运动手表、耳环等。

·201·

The referees decide what shall be considered dangerous. All protective equipment shall, if possible, be worn underneath the clothing. With the exception of elastic headbands without knots, no headgear may be worn. All forms of long tights are prohibited for field players. Exceptions shall be allowed only by the administrating authority upon written request.

406 Ball

The ball shall be approved by the IFF and marked accordingly.

407 Stick

1) The stick shall be approved by the IFF and marked accordingly.

All tampering with the shaft, except shortening, is prohibited. The shaft may be strapped above the grip mark, but no official marks may be covered.

2) The blade shall not be sharp and its hook shall not exceed 30 mm.

裁判有权裁定个人装备是否具危险性，所有防护装备尽可能穿戴在球衣内侧，除了有弹性的、没有打结的头饰，不得戴其他防护帽。场员禁止穿任何形式的长连裤袜，特例需书面请求主管方认可方可。

406 球

球必须经过IFF认证且具有相关标记。

407 球杆

1) 球杆必须经过IFF认证且具有相关标记。

除了缩短之外严禁任何改造，球杆上部可以包防滑带，但是不得覆盖官方标志。

2) 杆头不得为锋利材质且弯度不超过30毫米。

第六章　旱地冰球竞赛规则
Chapter Six　The Rules for Game

All tampering with the blade, except hooking, is prohibited. The hook shall be measured as the distance between the highest point of the blade's inner side and an even surface on which the stick is lying.

Changing the blade is allowed if the blade is approved with the shaft and being of the same brand, but the new blade shall not be weakened.

Taping the joint between the blade and the shaft is allowed, but no more than 10 mm of the visible part of the blade shall be covered.

408　The referees' equipment

The referees shall be equipped with plastic medium sized whistles, measuring equipment and red cards.

Exemption for other types of whistles may be given by the administrating authority.

除弯成钩状之外，严禁对杆头进行改造，球杆水平放置时，杆头弯部距离为杆头内侧最高点到水平面。

如杆头匹配，允许更换同一品牌杆头，但是新杆头不得被弱化。

可以在杆头和杆身之间使用胶带，但是覆盖杆头可见部分不得超过10毫米。

408　裁判装备

裁判员应备有中等大小的塑料口笛、测量设备和红牌，也可以使用其他主办方提供的可以发出哨声的设备。

409 The secretariat's equipment

The secretariat shall have all the equipment necessary for their responsibilities.

410 Control of equipment

1) The referees shall decide about controlling and measuring all equipment.

Inspection shall take place before and during the match. Incorrect equipment, including defective sticks measuring the stick's hook excluded, discovered before or during the match shall be corrected by the player concerned, who after this may start/continue the match.

Offences concerning players' uniforms and team captain's armlet shall not lead to more than one penalty per team per match.

However, all incorrect equipment shall be reported. No other players than the team

409 记录员装备

记录员应有其职责所需的所有必备设备。

410 装备的检查

1) 裁判员需要检查并测量所有的装备。

在赛前和赛中进行检查，不合规格装备，包括不合尺寸规定的球杆（无需测量球杆弯度），赛前或比赛中若有发现应予以更正，之后该球员方可开始或继续比赛。

球衣和队长袖标违规，每场比赛只需处罚一次。

但是，所有的不合规格装备都必须写入报告，在测

第六章　旱地冰球竞赛规则
Chapter Six　The Rules for Game

captains and the player with the equipment being measured may be at the secretariat during the measuring. After measuring, play shall be resumed according to what caused the interruption.

2)Measuring of a hook and control of a shaft/blade combination may be requested by the team captain.

The team captain also has the right to point out to the referees other incorrectness in the opponents' equipment, but in this case the referees decide whether or not to take action.

Measuring and control of shaft/blade combination may be requested at any time, but shall not be carried out until play is interrupted.

If control is requested during an interruption, it shall be carried out immediately, including in connection with goals and penalty shots, unless, in the referees'opinion, it negatively affects the situation

量装备期间，除队长和被测量队员外，其他人不得呆在记录席。测量结束后，比赛按之前局面重新开始。

2）球队队长可要求对弯钩、杆身及杆头结合处进行检查。

队长也有权向裁判指出对方其他的违规装备，但只有裁判可以决定是否采取行动。

针对球杆球头结合部的测量和检查可以在比赛的任何时段提出，但必须在比赛中断时进行。

如果检查要求发生在比赛中断的阶段，则应立即进行，包括在进球和罚球的阶段，除非裁判认为这会对对方球队产生不良的影响。这种情况下，检查在下一个比

·205·

for the opposing team. In this case the control shall be carried out at the next interruption.

The referees are obliged to check a hook or shaft/blade at the team captain's request, but only one control per team per interruption shall be allowed. No other players than the team captains and the player with the equipment being controlled may be at the secretariat during the measuring. After measuring, play shall be resumed according to what caused the interruption.

Section Five: Fixed Situations

501 General regulations for fixed situation

1)When play has been interrupted, it shall be resumed with a fixed situation, according to what caused the interruption.

Fixed situations are face-offs, hit-ins, free-hits and penalty shots.

赛中断时进行。

裁判有义务在队长申诉时检查球杆的弯钩、球杆和杆头,但是每队只允许一次中断、一次检查。在测量和检查期间,除了队长和持有该装备的队员,其他人不得呆在记录席,测量结束以后,比赛应根据之前的局面重新开始。

第五节　定位球

501 定位球的一般规则

1) 恢复被中断的比赛,应根据引起比赛中断的原因,按定位球的方式进行。

定位球包括争球、边线球、任意球和罚点球。

第六章　旱地冰球竞赛规则
Chapter Six　The Rules for Game

2)The referees shall use one signal, show prescribed signs and mark the place for the fixed situation. The ball may be played after the signal if it is not moving and is in the right position.

The referees shall first show the consequence sign and then a possible offence sign. The offence sign shall only be used if considered necessary, however always in connection with penalties and penalty shots.

If, in the referees' opinion, play is not affected, the ball does not have to be entirely still or in exactly the right place at a hit-in or a free-hit.

3)A fixed situation shall not be unreasonably delayed.

The referees decide what shall be considered unreasonable delay. If a fixed situation is delayed, the referees shall if possible notify the player before any action is taken.

502 Face-off (802)

1) At the start of a new period

2) 裁判需要做出定位球动作并确定发定位球的位置。如果球没有移动且处在正确位置，则在裁判示意后可以开球。

裁判应先做出判罚的手势，再做出可能的犯规判罚的手势，犯规判罚手势只有在裁判认为有必要的时候，一般是在处罚点球的情况下使用。

在边线球或任意球情况下，如果裁判认为没什么影响，球并不需要完全回到精确的位置。

3)定位球不得无故延误。

裁判判定何为无故延误，如果定位球被延误了，裁判应尽可能提前警告该队员。

502 争球（发球）(802)

1) 在新一节比赛开始或

·207·

and to confirm a correctly scored goal, a face-off shall be taken at the centre spot.

A goal scored during extra time, or from a penalty shot deciding the match, or after the end of a period, shall not be confirmed with a face-off.

When a face-off is taken at the centre spot, each team shall be on their own side of the centre line.

2) When play is interrupted and neither team can be awarded a hit-in, a free-hit or a penalty shot, play shall be resumed with a face-off.

3) A face-off shall be taken at the nearest face-off dot, according to where the ball was at the interruption.

4) All players, except those taking the face-off, shall immediately, without summons from the referees, take a position at least 3 m from the ball, sticks included.

者一个合法的进球得分之后，应该在中点争球。

加时赛进球、决定比赛结果的罚球、或一节结束之后，不必进行争球。

中点开球时，两队都必须处在本方的半场。

2）比赛中断但没有球队获得边线球、任意球或罚点球时，比赛应该从争球开始。

3）争球应根据比赛中断的地点选择最近的争球地点。

4）除参与争球的队员外，所有其他队员都应距球3米以上的距离（含球杆）。

第六章　旱地冰球竞赛规则
Chapter Six　The Rules for Game

Before a face-off, it is the referees' responsibility to check that the teams are ready and that all players have taken position.

5)A face-off shall be taken by one field player from each team. The players shall be facing the opposing team's short side and must not have physical contact before the face-off. The feet shall be placed perpendicular to the centre line. Each player shall have both his feet at the same distance from the centre line. The sticks shall be held with a normal grip and with both hands above the grip mark. The blades shall be placed perpendicular to the centre line on either side of the ball, but without touching it.

Normal grip implies the way the player holds his stick during play. The defending team's player chooses on which side of the ball to place his stick. If the face-off is on the centre line, the visiting team's player chooses. The ball shall be at the centres of the blades. If a player taking a face-

争球前，裁判有义务确认所有队员都处于其应在的位置。

5) 争球由两方各一名场员进行，该队员须面向对方半场的短边且与对方球员在开球前没有身体接触。两脚应垂直于中线，队员脚距中线距离都应相等，球杆两手正常握把并置于一定的高度，球杆头与中线垂直且置于球的两侧，但不能触球。

在争球过程中队员应保持正常握杆，球置于球杆头的中段。非中心点争球时，防守方队员可以选择将球杆放在球的哪一侧；如果争球在中线进行，则由客队队员选择。如果开球运动员不服从裁判的要求，则由另一名运

off does not obey the referees' instructions, another player who is on the rink shall take the face-off. In case of a dispute in connection with a substitution before a face-off is taken, the away team is obliged to carry out their substitution first.

6)A face-off may go directly into goal.

503 Events leading to a face-off

1)When the ball is damaged unintentionally.

2)When the ball is not correctly playable.

The referees shall, before interrupting play, give the players a reasonable opportunity to play the ball.

3)When parts of the board have been separated and the ball comes near the place in question.

4)When the goal cage is moved unintentionally and cannot be put back within a reasonable time.

动员开球，如果争球前换人，则客队有权率先进行换人。

6) 争球可以直接射门。

503 导致争球的局面

1) 球意外受损。

2)球不完全适用于比赛。

裁判在中断比赛前，给球员合理机会击球。

3) 当部分挡板断开，且球处于临近问题区域时。

4) 当球门被移动且无法在合适的时间内被复原。

第六章　旱地冰球竞赛规则
Chapter Six　The Rules for Game

It is the goalkeeper's responsibility to put the goal cage back as soon as this is considered possible.

5) When a serious injury occurs or an injured player directly affects play.

The referees decide what shall be considered a serious injury, but as soon as this is suspected, play shall be interrupted immediately.

6) When an unnatural situation occurs during play.

The referees decide what shall be considered an unnatural situation, but this always includes, amongst others, unauthorized persons or objects on the rink, the lights going out either completely or partly, and the final signal being sounded by mistake, or when a referee is hit by the ball and this has a significant effect on the play.

7) When a goal is disallowed despite the fact that no offence

守门员有义务在可能情况下迅速恢复球门原状。

5) 当发生严重伤害或者受伤队员直接影响了比赛时。

裁判判定什么是严重伤害，一旦有此怀疑，应立刻中断比赛。

6) 意外场面出现在比赛中时。

裁判有权认定什么是意外场面，一般包括未经许可的人或物体进入场地、照明完全或部分损坏、错误的终场信号、裁判被球击中且对比赛影响严重。

7) 尽管没有导致任意球的犯规状况，射门仍不算数时。

leading to a free-hit has been committed.

This includes when the ball goes into goal without passing the goal line from the front.

8) When a penalty shot does not result in a goal.

This includes when a penalty shot is incorrectly performed.

9) When a delayed penalty is carried out because the offending team gains and controls the ball.

This includes when the non-offending team, in the referees' opinion, is trying to waste time.

10) When a penalty is imposed for an offence which is not in connection with play, but is committed or noticed during play.

This includes when a penalized player enters the rink before his penalty expires or terminates.

11) When the referees are

例如当球进入球门但并没有从前门穿过球门线。

8) 点球没有进球时。

含点球没有正确执行。

9) 因犯规球队得球并控球需实施推迟处罚时。

包括裁判认为非犯规方故意拖延时间时。

10) 当处罚因非比赛直接相关的犯规引起，但该犯规在比赛中实施或被发现时。

例如受罚队员在处罚结束之前进入场地等。

11) 当裁判无法判定给

第六章　旱地冰球竞赛规则

Chapter Six　The Rules for Game

unable to decide the direction of a hit-in or a free-hit.

This includes when players from both teams commit offences simul-taneously.

12)When the referees' decision is considered incorrect.

This includes when the referees by mistake whistles for too many players and it shows that the team is playing without goalkeeper.

504 Hit-in (803)

1)When the ball leaves the rink, a hit-in shall be awarded to the non-offending team.

The offending team is considered to be the team whose player, or player's equipment, last touched the ball before it left the rink. This also includes when a player, to remove the ball from the goal cage, hits the net without touching the ball.

2)A hit-in shall be taken from where the ball leaves the

哪方边线球和任意球时。

包括两队队员同时犯规时。

12) 当裁判的判罚被认为是不正确时。

包括裁判误吹某队上场队员过多，而实际该队无人守门时。

504 边线球 (803)

1) 球出界时，未犯规队发边线球。

队员或队员的装备在球出界前最后碰触此球，则该队视为犯规队，包括将球从网中取出，虽未击球但击打球网导致球出界。

2) 边线球应当从球离开球场的位置实施，距离挡板

·213·

rink, 1.5 m from the board, but never behind the imaginary extensions of the goal lines.

If, in the referees' opinion, play is not affected, the ball does not have to be entirely still or in exactly the right place. If a team gets an advantage from taking a hit-in closer to the board than 1.5 m, this shall be allowed. A hit-in behind the imaginary extension of the goal line shall be taken from the nearest face-off dot. When the ball touches the ceiling or objects above the rink, the hit-in shall be taken 1.5 m from the board at the same distance from the centre line.

3)The opponents shall immediately, without summons from the referees, take a position at least 3 m from the ball, sticks included.

The player taking the hit-in does not have to wait for the opponents to take position, but if the ball is played while the opponents are trying to take

1.5米，但不能在球门线延长线后方。

如果裁判认为并不影响比赛，无需从精确位置争球，也允许某队距挡板不足1.5米处发边线球并获利。球门线延长线后面的边线球应从最近的争球点进行。当球触到球场上方天花板或物品时，边线球从距挡板1.5米且与中线同等距离处开球。

3）无需裁判要求其他队员与球保持3米以上距离（含球杆）。

发边线球时无需等待对方队员到位，但是当对方试图以合理方式采取正确的防守位置时，不应开球。

第六章　旱地冰球竞赛规则

Chapter Six　The Rules for Game

position in a correct way, no action shall be taken.

4)The ball shall be played with the stick. It shall be hit cleanly, not dragged, flicked or lifted on the stick.

5)The player taking the hit-in shall not touch the ball again before it has touched another player or another player's equipment.

6)A hit-in may go directly into goal.

505 Events leading to a hit-in

When the ball passes the board or hits the ceiling or any other object above the rink.

506 Free-hit (804)

1)When an offence leading to a free-hit is committed, a free-hit shall be awarded to the non-offending team. With offences leading to a free-hit, the advantage rule shall be applied whenever possible.

4) 用球杆击球，应当直接击打，禁止拖、轻碰或者以杆提起。

5) 边线球在接触另一个队员或其装备之前，负责开边线球的队员不得再次触球。

6) 边线球可以直接射门。

505 导致边线球的状况

球越过挡板或碰到场地上方天花板及其他物体时。

506 任意球(804)

1) 当犯规导致任意球时，任意球权利将给予未犯规球队，可能情况下实行保护进攻规则。

·215·

The advantage rule implies that if the non-offending team still controls the ball after an offence, they shall have the opportunity to go on playing if this gives them a greater advantage than a free-hit. If advantage is being played, and the game is interrupted because the non-offending team loses control of the ball, the resulting free-hit shall be placed where the original offence occurred.

2)The free-hit shall be taken where the offence was committed, but never behind the imaginary extensions of the goal lines, or closer to the goalkeeper areas than 3.5 m.

If, in the referees' opinion, play is not affected, the ball does not have to be entirely still or in exactly the right place. A free-hit closer to the board than 1.5 m may be moved out to this distance. A free-hit behind the imaginary extension of the goal line shall be taken from

当犯规导致任意球，应当尽可能实行保护进攻规则，包括如果未犯规队在被犯规后仍然控球，且情况比任意球更为有利，他们可以继续比赛；如未犯规队失去了控球权，则应在原犯规地点立即判罚任意球。

2) 任意球应在犯规发生的地点执行，但不能在球门线及其延长线后方，或者距守门员区3.5米内。

如果裁判认为不会影响比赛效果，任意球的地点可以并不精确在犯规的地点，如果任意球距挡板在1.5米之内，可移动至1.5米；球门线后方的任意球，可以移动到最近的争球点。距守门员区3.5米内的任意球必须移动

第六章　旱地冰球竞赛规则
Chapter Six　The Rules for Game

the nearest face-off dot. A free-hit closer to the goalkeeper area than 3.5 m shall be moved out to the distance of 3.5 m from the outer line of the goalkeeper area along an imaginary line from the centre of the goal line through the place where the offence was committed, leaving 0.5 m for the wall and then 3 meters free space to the free-hit point. In this case the defending team shall always have the right to form a defence line immediately outside their goalkeeper area. If the attacking team prevents or obstructs this, a free-hit shall be awarded to the defending team. The attacking team is not obliged to wait for the defending team to form the defence line, and has the right to place their players in front of the defence line.

3)The opponents shall immediately, without summons from the referees, take a position at least 3 m from the ball, sticks included.

到中轴线距球门区外线3.5米处，距人墙0.5米。此时防守队员在守门员区外可以组成人墙，距离任意球点至少3米。如果进攻队对此作出妨碍，则由防守队发任意球；进攻队无需等待防守队组好人墙，同样也可以在人墙前面布置本方队员。

3) 无需裁判员要求，对方队员应与球保持3米以上的距离（包括球杆）。

The player taking the free-hit does not have to wait for the opponents to take position, but if the ball is played while the opponents are trying to take position in a correct way, no action shall be taken.

4)The ball shall be played with the stick. It shall be hit properly, not dragged, flicked or lifted on the stick.

5)The player taking the free-hit shall not touch the ball again before it has touched another player or another player's equipment.

6)A free-hit may go directly into goal.

507 Offences leading to a free-hit

1)When a player hits, blocks, lifts, kicks an opponent's stick or holds an opponent or opponent's stick (901, 902, 903, 910, 912).

If the referees consider the

任意球的队员无需等待防守队员就位，但是当对方试图以合理方式采取正确的防守位置时，不做开球。

4) 球应用球杆击打，应直接击打，禁止拖、轻碰或以杆提起。

5) 任意球在接触另一个队员或者其装备之前，打任意球的队员不得再次触球。

6) 任意球可以直接射门。

507 导致任意球的犯规

1) 当一名队员击打、阻碍、提起、踢对手的球杆或者握住对方的球杆，抓住对手或其球杆（901，902，903，910，912）。

如果裁判员认为在击中

第六章　旱地冰球竞赛规则
Chapter Six　The Rules for Game

player to have played the ball before hitting the opponent's stick, no action shall be taken.

2)When a field player raises the blade of his stick above waist level in the back swing before hitting the ball, or in the forward swing after hitting the ball(904).

This includes mock shots. A high forward swing is allowed if no other players are in the vicinity, and there is no risk of injury. As waist level is considered the level of the waist when standing upright.

3) When a field player uses any part of his stick or his foot, to play or try to play the ball above knee level (904, 913).

Stopping the ball with a thigh is not considered to be playing the ball above knee level, unless considered dangerous. As knee level is considered the level of the knees when standing upright.

4)When a field player

对方球杆前已经触到了球，则不做任何判罚。

2) 当一名场员将在击球前或击球后，球杆举过腰部（904）。

包括模拟击球。如果附近没有其他队员且不会引发伤害允许向前挥杆高举。腰的高度以人正常站立为准。

3) 当场员使用球杆的任何部位或脚，来接触或试图接触高于膝盖的球（904,913）。

用大腿停球不被认为是膝盖高抬触球，除非被认定为危险动作，膝盖的高度也以正常站立为准。

4) 当队员把球杆、腿或

places his stick, his foot or his leg between an opponent's legs or feet(905).

5)When a player, in control of the ball, or trying to reach it, forces or pushes an opponent in any way other than shoulder to shoulder (907).

6)When a player, in control of the ball, trying to reach it, or trying to get a better position, moves backwards into an opponent, or prevents an opponent from moving in the direction intended (908, 911).

This includes when the attacking team prevents or obstructs the formation of a defence line at a free hit awarded within 3.5 m of the goalkeeper's area.

7)When a field player kicks the ball twice, unless in between it has touched the player's stick, another player or another player's equipment(912).

This shall be considered

脚伸到对方队员的腿或脚间（905）。

5）当队员在控球或尝试接球时，以肩碰肩之外的任何方式挤或推对方队员时（907）。

6）当一名队员正在控球，尝试获取更好的位置，后移撞到对手，或阻止对手向拟定方向移动（908，911）。

包括任意球时进攻方阻碍对方在球门区3.5米内形成人墙防线。

7）当一名场员两次踢球时（踢球间隙球触杆、触另外队员或另外队员装备时除外）(912)。

如果裁判认为该队员两

第六章　旱地冰球竞赛规则
Chapter Six　The Rules for Game

an offence only if the player, in the referees'opinion, both times kicks the ball intentionally.

8)When a player receives a foot pass from a field player in the same team(912).

This shall be considered an offence only if the pass, in the referees'opinion, is intentional.

Receiving a foot pass from a player in the same team is allowed if an opponent omits to take the ball despite the possibility to do so. A foot pass to the goalkeeper is not considered a goal situation and can't result in a penalty shot.

9)When a field player is in the goalkeeper area(914).

A field player is allowed to pass through the goalkeeper area if, in the referees'opinion, play is not affected and the goalkeeper's actions are not hindered.

If, when a free-hit for the opposing team is hit directly

次都是故意踢球，则判其犯规。

8) 当队员接收到了同队场员的脚传球（912）。

只有当裁判认为是故意传球的时候，才判罚犯规。

在对方可能失误的情况下接到同队队员的脚传球是可以的，脚传球给守门员不能视为射门，也不必罚球。

9) 当场员位于守门员区（914）。

如果裁判认为并不会阻碍守门员的防守，场员可以通过守门员区。

如果进攻方的任意球直接射门时，防守方的场员在

at the goal, a field player of the defending team is in the goalkeeper area, in the goal cage or, if the goal cage has been moved, in the area where the goal cage normally stands, a penalty shot shall always be awarded.

A field player is considered to be in the goalkeeper area if any part of his body touches the floor inside the goalkeeper area. A field player with only his stick in the goalkeeper area is not considered to be in the goalkeeper area. The lines belong to the goalkeeper area.

10)When a field player intentionally moves the opposing team's goal cage.(914)

11)When a field player passively obstructs the goal-keeper's throw-out(915).

This shall be considered an offence only if the field player is inside the goal crease or closer to the goalkeeper than 3 m, measured from where the goalkeeper gains control

守门员区内、在球门处，或球门被移离正常区，则通常会判罚点球。

场员身体的任何部分碰触守门员区场地内，则被视为在守门员区内，但如果只有球杆在内，则不被认为在守门员区内。球门线含在球门区内。

10) 当场员有意移动对手的球门时（914）。

11) 当场员被动阻碍守门员的手抛球（915）。

只有当场员在球门区内或距守门员3米以内（以守门员控球的位置为准），且守门员可以控制到球，移动示为非故意或大意移动。

第六章　旱地冰球竞赛规则
Chapter Six　The Rules for Game

of the ball. Passively implies unintentionally or through omission to move.

12)When a field player jumps up and stops the ball(916).

As jumping is considered to be when both feet entirely leave the floor. Running is not considered as jumping. A player is allowed to jump over the ball if he does not touch it.

13)When a field player plays the ball from outside the rink (no offence sign).

Outside implies having one or both feet outside the rink. If a player plays the ball from outside the rink during substitution, this shall be considered too many players on the rink. If a player, not in the process of changing, plays the ball from the substitution zone, this shall be considered sabotage of play.

It is allowed to run outside the rink, but the ball shall not be played from there.

12) 当场员跳起停球时（916）。

跳是指两只脚都离开了地面，奔跑不被认定为是跳跃，如果队员不触球，可以跳过球。

13) 当场员在场外进行比赛（无犯规标志）。

场外是指一脚或两脚在场地之外，如在换人时，队员在场外进行比赛，将被认为是超员进行比赛，如果非替换过程中的队员从休息区触球，则被认为是蓄意破坏比赛。

允许跑到场外，但是不能在场外触球。

14)When a goalkeeper entirely leaves the goal crease during a throw-out(917).

In this case the goalkeeper is not considered a field player. The goalkeeper is considered to have entirely left the goal crease when no part of his body touches the floor in the goal crease. The throw-out is completed when the goalkeeper lets go of the ball, and if he leaves the goal crease after this, no action shall be taken.

This rule shall also apply if the goalkeeper gathers the ball inside the goal crease and his entire body then slides outside the goal crease.

The lines belong to the goal crease.

15)When a goalkeeper throws or kicks the ball over the centre line (917).

This shall be considered an offence only if the ball does not touch the floor, the board, another player or another player's equipment before it passes the

14）守门员完全离开球门区手抛球时(917)。

这种情况下这名守门员不作为场员。当守门员身体任何部分都没有接触球门区场地时，认定其离开了球门区。如果在手抛球之后离开了球门区，则不作任何判罚。

这一规定同样适用于守门员在球门区内得球然后滑到球门区外。

球门线含在球门区内。

15) 当守门员将球抛过或踢过中线（917）。

只有当球未经碰触地面、挡板、其他队员或队员装备直接越过中线时，才被认为是犯规，且必须是整个

第六章 旱地冰球竞赛规则
Chapter Six The Rules for Game

centre line. The entire ball has to pass the centre line.

16)When a face-off, hit-in or a free-hit is incorrectly performed or intentionally delayed(918).

This includes when the non-offending team takes the ball away when the play is interrupted, the ball is dragged, flicked, or lifted on the stick. If a hit-in or a free-hit is taken from the wrong place or when the ball is not entirely still, it may be taken again. If, in the referees' opinion, play is not affected, the ball does not have to be entirely still or in exactly the right place.

17)When a goalkeeper has the ball under control for more than 3 seconds(924).

If the goalkeeper puts the ball down and picks it up again this shall be considered controlling the ball all the time.

18)When a goalkeeper receives a pass from a field player in the same team (924).

球越过中线方可。

16) 争球、边线球或者任意球被错误的执行或故意延误时（918）。

包括未犯规队在比赛中断时将球带走，用球杆拖拽、轻敲、拖拉球。如边线球或者任意球在错误的地点发出，或球未停稳应重发。如果裁判认为并不影响比赛进程，则无需放到精确的位置或完全停稳。

17) 守门员控球超过3秒（924）。

如果守门员把球放下又拿起来，视作一直在持球。

18) 当守门员接受同队场员的传球（924）。

This shall be considered an offence only if the pass, in the referees' opinion, is intentional. Receiving implies that the goalkeeper touches the ball with either his hands or arms, also even after the goalkeeper has possibly touched or stopped the ball with any other part of his body.

A goalkeeper may receive a pass from a player in the same team if the goalkeeper is completely outside his goal crease when he receives the pass, and is thereby considered a field player.

If the goalkeeper leaves his goal crease entirely, stops the ball, returns to his goal crease and picks the ball up this shall not be considered a pass to the goalkeeper.

A pass to the goalkeeper is not considered a goal situation and cannot result in a penalty shot.

19)When a penalty is

只有当裁判认为这是一种故意行为时才算犯规。接球意味着守门员用任一只手或者手臂接触球，或者用身体的其他部分接触球。

守门员可以接受同队场员的传球，此时守门员应完全在球门区之外，被视为一名场员。

如果守门员完全离开球门区，停球、回到球门区，用手将球拿起，不能被视为传球给守门员。

向守门员传球不被认作是射门则不能导致罚球。

19) 当犯规与比赛有关

Chapter Six   The Rules for Game

imposed for an offence committed in connection with play. (prescribed offence sign)

20)When a player delays play (924).

This includes when a field player, in order to waste time, places himself against the rink or goal cage in such a manner that the opponent is unable to reach the ball in a correct way. The player should, if possible, be made aware of this before any actions are taken.

508 Penalty shot (806)

1)When an offence leading to a penalty shot is committed, a penalty shot shall be awarded to the non-offending team.

If a penalty shot is awarded during a delayed penalty or caused by an offence leading to a penalty, the rules concerning penalties in connection with a penalty shot shall also be applied.

2) The penalty shot shall be taken from the centre spot.

时的判罚（犯规标志）。

20) 当队员拖延比赛时(924)。

包括场员拖延时间，将自身置于场地或球门附近导致对方无法以合适的方式接触球，该球员在被判罚前应受到警告。

508 罚球 (806)

1) 足以导致罚球的犯规被认定时，将给予未犯规球队罚球权。

如果延迟罚点球又引发了一次犯规，或又一次犯规引起判罚，仍应再次判罚点球。

2）罚点球应从中心点开始。

3)All players except the player taking the penalty shot and the defending goalkeeper shall be in their substitution zones during the entire penalty shot. The goalkeeper shall be on the goal line when the penalty shot starts.

The goalkeeper must not be replaced by a field player. If the goalkeeper commits an offence during the penalty shot, a new penalty shot shall be awarded and any prescribed penalty carried out. If another player in the offending team commits an offence during the penalty shot, a new penalty shot shall be awarded and the offence considered sabotage of play.

4)The player taking the penalty shot may play the ball an unlimited number of times, but the ball has to be in a forward movement during the entire penalty shot. As soon as the goalkeeper has touched the ball, the player taking the penalty shot must not touch the ball again

3) 除罚球的球员及守门员外所有队员都应在休息区。罚球前守门员必须位于球门线。

守门员不可由场员替代，如守门员在罚球期间犯规，则需追加一次规定的罚点球，如果犯规队的其他队员在罚球过程中有犯规，追加新的罚点球，且该犯规被认为是蓄意破坏比赛。

4) 罚点球的球员可以无限次触球，但是罚点球期间必须向前移动球。一旦守门员触球，负责罚球的队员就不能再次碰球。

第六章 旱地冰球竞赛规则
Chapter Six The Rules for Game

during the penalty shot.

Game time shall be stopped during the entire penalty shot. Forward movement implies away from the centre line. If the ball hits the front face of the goal then the goalkeeper, and passes the goal line from the front, the goal shall be allowed. If the ball at the very start of a penalty shot is drawn backwards the penalty shot shall be interrupted and started all over again.

5) A 2 minute bench penalty imposed in connection with a penalty shot shall be noted in the match record only if the penalty shot does not result in a goal.

The penalized player shall be on the penalty bench during the penalty shot.

509 Delayed penalty shot (807)

1) A delayed penalty shot shall be applied when the non-offending team still controls the ball after an offence leading

罚球期间，应停止计时，向前移动即为远离中线，如果球触及球门的前端，碰到守门员，并从正面越过球门线，进球有效。如果罚点球时球退后，则应重新罚球。

5) 只有当罚球没有形成进球时，罚点球而致的2分钟退场处罚需记录在案。

罚点球时被判罚球员应坐在判罚席上。

509 延迟罚点球(807)

1) 当未犯规队仍有控球权，同时正在对球门形成进攻的时候，应当作出延迟罚球的判罚。

to a penalty shot, and the goal situation is still in progress.

If a delayed penalty shot is awarded during a delayed penalty or caused by an offence leading to a penalty, the rules concerning penalties in connection with a penalty shot shall also be applied. A delayed penalty shot may be caused by an offence leading to a penalty even if a delayed penalty is already in progress.

2)A delayed penalty shot implies that the non-offending team is given the possibility to continue the attack until the immediate goal situation is over.

A delayed penalty shot shall still be carried out after the end of a period or a match. If the non-offending team scores correctly during a delayed penalty shot, the goal shall be allowed and the penalty shot cancelled.

如果延迟罚点球又引发了一次犯规，或又一次犯规引起判罚，仍应再次判罚点球。即使已经处于推迟罚球的过程中，仍可能由一次导致罚球的犯规引发再次罚点球。

2) 延迟罚点球意味着未犯规球队可以持续攻击，直到最后射门结束为止。

一节比赛或整场比赛结束后仍应执行顺延罚球，如果未犯规队在推迟罚球期间直接得分，则推迟的罚球可以取消。

第六章　旱地冰球竞赛规则
Chapter Six　The Rules for Game

510　Offences leading to a penalty shot

When a goal situation is interrupted, or prevented from occurring, because the defending team has committed an offence leading to a free-hit or a penalty. (prescribed offence sign)

　　The referees decide what shall be considered a goal situation. Offences in the goal crease shall not automatically lead to a penalty shot.

　　A penalty shot shall always be awarded when the defending team, during a goal situation, intentionally moves the goal cage or intentionally plays with too many players on the rink.

　　If, when a free-hit for the opposing team is hit directly at the goal, a field player of the defending team is in the goalkeeper area, in the goal cage or, if the goal cage has been moved, in the area where the goal cage normally stands, a penalty shot shall always be awarded.

510　导致罚点球的犯规

　　当防守队员犯规可致任意球或罚点球打断或阻止一个进球机会时（按犯规规定）。

　　裁判认定什么是进球的机会，在球门区的犯规不会自动导致罚点球。

　　一般当防守队故意移动球门或过多队员上场，被视为破坏一次进球机会，应判罚球。

　　如果对方任意球直接射门时，防守方的场员在守门员区内及球门内或将球门移离正常位置时，应判罚点球。

·231·

Section Six: Penalties

601 General regulations for penalties

1) When an offence leading to a penalty is committed, the offender shall be penalized.

If the referees are unable to point out the offender, or if the offence is committed by a member of the team staff, the team captain shall choose a field player, who is not already penalized, to serve the penalty. If the team captain refuses to do this, or is penalized, the referees shall choose the player.

All penalties carried out shall be noted in the match record with the time, number of the player, type of penalty and cause of penalty. If the penalty is caused by an offence in connection with play, the non-offending team shall be awarded a free-hit.

第六节 处罚

601 处罚的一般规则

1) 当犯规导致判罚时，犯规者应受到处罚。

如果裁判无法指明犯规者，或犯规由某名球队工作人员引发，球队队长须选择一名尚未受到处罚的队员来接受处罚。若队长拒绝，或正在接受处罚，则由裁判选定受罚队员。

所有处罚须在记录纸上注明时间、队员号码、处罚的种类及原因。如处罚因比赛中行为引起，则未犯规方可获任意球。

第六章　旱地冰球竞赛规则
Chapter Six　The Rules for Game

If the penalty is caused by an offence not in connection with play, play shall be resumed with a face-off.

如果处罚并非因比赛中行为引起，则重新争球继续比赛。

If the penalty is caused by an offence committed during an interruption, play shall be resumed according to what caused the interruption.

如果处罚由比赛中断阶段的行为引起，则比赛将从引发中断的局面继续开始。

A penalized team captain loses his right to speak to the referees, unless he is addressed by them.

受罚队长无权与裁判进行对话，除非他被要求对话。

2)A penalized player shall be on the penalty bench during the entire penalty.

2) 受罚队员在整个受罚阶段都应位于处罚席。

All penalties terminate when the match is over. A penalty, which has not expired at the end of regular game time, shall continue during extra time. A penalized player shall be on the same side of the centre line as his team, with the exception of when the secretariat and the penalty benches are situated on the same side of the rink as the substitution zones.

比赛结束所有未结束的处罚视同结束。如处罚在常规时间没有结束，则应该延续计时到加时赛。受罚队员应和球队在同一侧的处罚席。除非记录席与休息区均在同一侧。

· 233 ·

北欧时尚运动——旱地冰球
Nordic Fashion Sport FLOORBALL

During regular game time a penalized player may leave the penalty bench during an intermission. A penalized player shall not leave the penalty bench during the intermission between regular game time and extra time. A penalized player is not allowed to participate in a time out. A player, whose penalty expires, shall immediately leave the penalty bench, unless the number of penalties for his team makes this impossible or the penalty expiring is a personal penalty. A goalkeeper, whose penalty expires, shall not leave the penalty bench until the next interruption.

A penalized player who is injured may be replaced on the penalty bench by a field player who is not already penalized. Both players shall be noted in the match record with the number of the player actually serving the penalty in brackets. If the injured player enters the rink before the penalty expires, match penalty one will be imposed.

节间休息时，受罚队员可以离开处罚席，但在常规时间和加时赛中间，受罚队员不能离开处罚席。受罚队员不能参与暂停。处罚期满的队员，必须立刻离开处罚席，除非受球队受罚队员人数所限或者受到的是一次个人处罚。处罚期满的守门员，直到下一次比赛中断才可以离开处罚席。

被处罚的球员受伤，可以由一名未受处罚的队员更换。这两名球员在比赛中都应当在记录中标明（括号中列明真正犯规队员），如果受伤选手处罚期满之前回到场内，将被处以第一类罚离场处罚。

第六章　旱地冰球竞赛规则
Chapter Six　The Rules for Game

If the secretariat is responsible for a player being admitted to the rink too soon and the mistake is noticed during regular penalty time, the player shall resume his position on the penalty bench. There shall not be any additional penalty time and the player shall return to the rink when his regular penalty time expires.

3)If a goalkeeper incurs one or several 2 minute bench penalties, the team captain shall choose a field player, who is not already penalized, to serve the penalty.

A goalkeeper incurring a 5 minute bench penalty or a personal penalty shall serve the penalty himself.

If a goalkeeper incurs one or several 2 minutes bench penalties when serving penalties or in connection with a 5 minute bench penalty or a personal penalty, he shall serve these penalties himself.

如果记录员允许队员过快回到场地，则应该予以提出并要求队员回到处罚席。当处罚期满之后，不必有任何追加处罚。

3) 如守门员引发一个或几个2分钟的判罚席处罚，该队队长可以选择一个未受罚的场员来接受处罚。

如守门员招致5分钟判罚席处罚或个人处罚，则由本人受罚。

如守门员在受罚期间引发了一个或几个2分钟退场处罚，或与5分钟退场处罚及个人处罚有关的处罚，他需要自己接受这些处罚。

If a goalkeeper serves penalties and a reserve goalkeeper is not available, the team has a maximum of 3 minutes to properly equip a field player, but none of this time shall be used for warming up. The new goalkeeper shall be marked in the match record, and the time of the change shall be noted.

When the penalty expires, the goalkeeper must not enter the rink until play is interrupted. Due to this the team captain shall choose a field player, who is not already penalized, to accompany the goalkeeper on the penalty bench in order to enter the rink when the penalty expires. Only the penalized player shall be noted in the match record. The referees shall together with the secretariat help a goalkeeper, whose penalty has expired during play, to leave the penalty bench as soon as play is interrupted.

4)Penalty time shall be synchronized to game time.

如守门员受罚且没有替补守门员，则球队有最多3分钟装备场员作为守门员，无热身时间。记录纸上面标明新守门员及更换时间。

处罚期满后，守门员在比赛中断后才能进入场地。鉴于此，队长可以选择一名未受罚的场员在处罚席陪伴守门员，以备处罚期满后守门员可进入场地。只有受罚队员需要在记录纸上标明，裁判应当与记录员一起协助受罚守门员在处罚期满之后比赛中断时尽快返回场地。

4) 处罚时间应与比赛时间保持同步。

第六章　旱地冰球竞赛规则
Chapter Six　The Rules for Game

602　Bench penalty

1)A bench penalty shall affect the team, and due to this the penalized player shall not be replaced on the rink during the penalty.

2)No more than one bench penalty per player and two bench penalties per team shall be measured simultaneously.

All bench penalties shall be measured in the order they are imposed. A player, whose penalty cannot be measured, shall be on the penalty bench from the moment his penalty is carried out.

If more than one penalty is imposed simultaneously on a team already having a bench penalty, the team captain decides which of the new penalties shall be measured first. Shorter bench penalties shall, in this case, always be measured before longer.

602　退场处罚

1) 退场处罚对球队影响大，受罚期间受罚队员不得被替换上场。

2) 每名队员不同时接受两次退场处罚，每队同时最多有两名队员接受退场处罚。

所有的退场处罚均需按照次序执行，某名队员当处罚无法确定时，必须从他处罚执行开始就进入处罚席。

如某队同时受到两个退场处罚，则队长有权决定哪个处罚先被执行，一般短时间的处罚在长时间处罚之前执行。

3)A team, which has more than two players with carried out bench penalties, shall still have the right to play with four players on the rink.

The team shall play with four players on the rink until they have only one bench penalty being measured.

A player, whose bench penalty expires before this, shall remain on the penalty bench until play is interrupted or, if this occurs sooner, further bench penalties expire so that his team has only one bench penalty being measured. All penalized players in a team shall leave the penalty bench in the same order as their bench penalties expire, but the rules concerning the number of players allowed on the rink shall be noticed all the time. The referees, together with the secretariat, shall help a player, whose penalty has expired during play, to leave the penalty bench as soon as play is interrupted.

3)一个球队如果有两名队员受退场处罚，4名队员依然可以进行比赛。

球队继续比赛直至只剩一个退场处罚被执行。

受罚期在比赛中断前结束，该队员应留在处罚席直到比赛中断；如果中断较早，进一步处罚期满，这样他的球队只剩一个退场处罚在执行。球队中所有被罚球员按退场处罚期满顺序离开处罚席，但应时刻注意场上允许的队员数量之规则。比赛一中断，裁判和记录员一起帮助比赛进行中处罚期满的球员尽快离开处罚席。

第六章　旱地冰球竞赛规则
Chapter Six　The Rules for Game

4)If a player, who has incurred a bench penalty, commits further offences leading to a penalty, all his penalties shall be served consecutively.

This is regardless of whether the first penalty has started or not.

If a bench penalty has already started and the same player incurs another penalty, the measuring of the first penalty shall not be affected, but go on from where it was when the new penalty was carried out.

Consecutively implies that as soon as the player's first bench penalty expires or terminates, the next one shall start being measured, unless the team has other bench penalties, not yet being measured, which have been imposed in between the first player's bench penalties.

An unlimited number of bench penalties can be imposed on the same player. If a player

4) 如果退场球员在接受处罚时又有犯规行为，所有处罚应连续执行。

无需考虑第一个处罚是否已开始执行。

如退场处罚开始，但该队员导致了另一个处罚，第一次处罚不受影响，从新处罚执行时继续。

连续意味着一旦退场球员的第一个处罚期满或终止后，下一个处罚立即开始。两个处罚之间球队有其他未执行的退场处罚除外。

同一队员可被数次处以退场处罚。如果一个球员引致个人犯规，所有他退场处

has incurred a personal penalty, all his bench penalties have to expire or terminate before the personal penalty may start to be measured.

If a player is serving a personal penalty, then incurs a bench penalty, the measuring of the remaining personal penalty shall, as soon as the bench penalty can be measured, be postponed until the bench penalty expires or terminates. The team captain shall choose a field player, who is not already penalized, to accompany the player on the penalty bench in order to enter the rink when the bench penalty expires.

If a penalized player commits an offence leading to a match penalty, the rules concerning match penalties shall also be applied.

603 2 minute bench penalty

1) If the opposing team scores during a 2 minute bench penalty that is being measured,

罚期满或终止后才执行个人处罚。

如球员先受到个人处罚后导致退场处罚，一旦退场处罚可被执行，个人处罚则被延迟到退场处罚到期或终止时。队长可以选择一名未被处罚的队员在处罚席上陪伴受罚队员，以便处罚期满后，尽快回到比赛中来。

如被罚队员的犯规导致了比赛惩罚，则应按比赛惩罚执行。

603 2分钟退场处罚

1) 如果对方在2分钟退场处罚的执行期间得分，则

第六章　旱地冰球竞赛规则
Chapter Six　The Rules for Game

the penalty shall terminate, unless the opposing team is outnumbered on the rink or the teams play with equal strength.

The penalty will not terminate if the goal is scored neither during a delayed penalty nor from a penalty shot caused by an offence leading to a penalty.

2)If a team has more than one 2 minute bench penalty, these shall terminate in the same order they have been carried out.

604 Delayed penalty

1)All penalties may be delayed. A delayed penalty shall be applied when the non-offending team still controls the ball after an offence leading to a penalty. Only one penalty at a time can be delayed except when a goal situation is in progress, in which case a second penalty may also be delayed.

If one or several delayed penalties are imposed in connection with a penalty shot

处罚应被终止，除非得球队人数少或双方球队人数等同。

如果得分既不在延迟处罚期，也不是因犯规引起的罚点球所致，则处罚不得终止。

2) 如果球队不止有一个2分钟退场处罚，则应该按照执行次序依次结束。

604 延迟处罚

1) 所有处罚都可能被推迟。延迟处罚应用于未违规球队在遭遇导致罚球的犯规之后仍然控制球时。一次只能执行一次推迟处罚，除非射门进行中，在此情况下，可能形成第二个推迟处罚。

如果一个或几个延迟处罚引致罚点球或延迟罚点球，则犯规引起的罚点球规

· 241 ·

or a delayed penalty shot, the rules concerning penalties in connection with a penalty shot shall also be applied.

2) A delayed penalty implies that the non-offending team is given the possibility to continue the attack until the offending team gains and controls the ball or play is interrupted.

During a delayed penalty, the non-offending team shall be given the opportunity to replace the goalkeeper with a field player and continue the attack. A delayed penalty shall still be carried out after the end of a period or a match. If the delayed penalty is carried out because the offending team gains and controls the ball, play shall be resumed with a face-off.

The non-offending team shall use a delayed penalty for constructive attacking play. If the referees consider the team only to be trying to waste time, the players shall be notified.

则适用。

2) 延迟罚球应用于未犯规球队可以继续进攻时，直到犯规队得球或比赛中断止。

在延迟处罚中，未犯规球队有机会以一名场员替换守门员并继续进攻，延迟处罚仍可以在一节或正常比赛结束后执行。如果因进攻队得球或控球而实行延迟处罚，则比赛应从争球重新开始。

未犯规队应当有效利用延迟处罚组织进攻，如果裁判认为球队只是在试图浪费时间，则应警告队员。

第六章　旱地冰球竞赛规则
Chapter Six　The Rules for Game

If the team still does not try to attack, play shall be interrupted, the delayed penalty carried out and play resumed with a face-off.

If the delayed penalty is carried out because of any other interruption, play shall be resumed according to what caused the interruption.

If the non-offending team scores in a correct way during a delayed penalty, the goal shall be allowed and the delayed 2 minute bench penalty last imposed on the team shall not be carried out. No other penalties shall be affected.

If the offending team scores during a delayed penalty, the goal shall be disallowed and play resumed with a face-off.

If the non-offending team scores an own goal, the goal shall be allowed.

如果球队依旧不尝试进攻，则比赛中止，实行延迟处罚并进行争球。

如果因其他比赛中断而致延迟处罚，则比赛应由引起中断时局面开始。

如果未犯规球队在推迟罚球阶段以正确方式得分，进球有效，推迟的2分钟退场处罚不再处罚，其他处罚照旧。

如果延迟处罚阶段犯规队得分，进球视作无效，且比赛从争球开始。

如果未犯规队进了一个乌龙球，则进球有效。

• 243 •

605 Offences leading to a 2 minute bench penalty

1)When a player, hits, blocks, lifts, kicks an opponent's stick or holds an opponent or opponent's stick in order to win a considerable advantage, or with no possibility of reaching the ball(901, 902, 903, 910, 912).

2)When a field player plays the ball above waist level with any part of his stick or his foot(904, 913).

As waist level is considered the level of the player's waist when standing upright.

3)When a player is guilty of dangerous play with the stick (904).

This includes uncontrolled forward or backward swing of the stick, and raising the stick above an opponent's head if this is considered dangerous or disturbing for the opponent.

605 导致2分钟退场处罚的犯规

1) 当球员为从中得利或者无法得球的情况下，打、踢、抬起、阻碍对手球杆，拉对手或其球杆时（901、902、903、910、912）。

2) 当球员用球杆或脚的任何部分触球超过腰部时（904,913）。

腰高为球员正常站立时腰的高度。

3) 当球员用球杆做出危险动作（904）。

包括向前或向后无限挥杆，举杆高过对方头顶等其他危险的干扰动作。

第六章　旱地冰球竞赛规则
Chapter Six　The Rules for Game

4)When a player forces or pushes an opponent against the board or the goal cage (907).

5)When a player tackles or trips an opponent (909).

6)When a team captain requests measuring of a hook or control of the shaft/blade combination and the controlled equipment is correct (no offence sign).

The team captain will serve the penalty.

7)When a field player participates in play without a stick (no offence sign).

This does not include a goalkeeper, temporarily considered a field player.

8)When a field player fetches a stick from a place other than the team's own substitution zone (no offence sign).

9) When a field player omits to pick up his broken or dropped stick from the rink and bring it to his substitution zone.

4) 球员用力推挤对方至挡板或球门时（907）。

5) 球员铲或者踢打对手（909）。

6) 当某队长要求检查对方杆头弯钩或杆与杆头连接处而检查结果并未违规，该队长须受罚（无犯规标志）。

7) 当一个场员在比赛中未持球杆(无犯规标志)。

不包括守门员暂时被认为是场员的情况。

8) 当球员没有从自己的休息区取球杆时（无犯规标志）。

9) 当球员拒绝从场地捡起其破损或掉落球杆并带回到己方休息区时。

Only clearly visible parts of the stick have to be removed by the player.

10) When a player intentionally moves to obstruct an opponent, who is not in control of the ball(911).

If a player who is trying to move into a better position backs into an opponent, or prevents an opponent from moving in the direction intended, only a free-hit shall be awarded.

11) When a field player actively obstructs the goalkeeper's throw-out(915).

This shall be considered an offence only if the field player is inside the goal crease or closer to the goalkeeper than 3 m, measured from where the goalkeeper gains control of the ball. Actively implies following the goalkeeper sideways or trying to reach the ball with the stick.

12) When a player violates the 3 m rule at a hit-in or a free-

移除球杆明显可见部分。

10) 当场员故意移动阻碍对方未控球的球员(911)。

如球员正试图移动到更好的位置撞到对方，或阻止对方向拟定方向移动，只能判罚任意球。

11) 场上队员主动干扰守门员的手抛球（915）。

此时该球员在球门区内或距守门员持球位置3米以内，主动干扰即随守门员移动或者用球杆试图触球。

12) 队员在边线球和任意球局面下违背了3米规则

第六章　旱地冰球竞赛规则
Chapter Six　The Rules for Game

hit(915).

If the hit-in or the free-hit is performed while the opponents are trying to take position in a correct way, no action shall be taken. If a team forms a defence line which is not at a proper distance, only one player shall be penalized.

13)When a field player stops or plays the ball when lying or sitting down(919).

This also includes stopping or playing the ball with both knees, or one hand, on the floor, stick holding hand excluded.

14)When a field player stops or plays the ball with his hand, arm or head(920, 921).

15)When an incorrect substitution takes place (922).

The player leaving the rink has to be passing over the board before a new player may enter the rink. If the case is close, action shall only be taken if play is affected. It is also incorrect

（915）。

如果对方球员尝试正确站位，发边线球或任意球时，不需判罚。如果防守队的人墙不在合理距离内，只判罚一名队员。

13）当队员躺着或者坐着停球或打球时（919）。

也包括用双膝、单手、躺在地板上停球或打球，但不包括持杆的手。

14）当场员用头、手、手臂停球或打球(920, 921)。

15）当发生不正确换人时（922）。

当被替换队员越过挡板后，替换队员才可进入场地，如果动作非常接近，不影响比赛的前提下，可以不做判罚。同样当比赛中断

substitution when a player changes outside the team's own substitution zone when play is interrupted. The player entering the rink is the one to be penalized.

16) When a team plays with too many players on the rink (922).

Only one player shall be penalized.

17) When a penalized player:

Without entering the rink, leaves the penalty bench before his penalty expires or terminates.

Refuses to leave the penalty bench when his penalty expires.

Enters the rink during an interruption in the game, before his penalty expires or terminates(925).

The secretariat shall notify the referees of this as soon as possible. A player, whose penalty expires, shall not leave the penalty bench if the number

时，队员不在本方休息区进行交换也视为不正当换人，上场的球员应受到处罚。

16) 在场人数超额时（922）。

只可处罚一名队员。

17) 受罚队员出现以下状况时：

在处罚时间结束前离开处罚席但并没有进入场地；

在处罚时间结束后，拒绝离开处罚席；

在处罚时间结束或终止前，在比赛中断时进入场地（925）。

记录员应立刻通知裁判这些情况。因球队处罚次数导致他不能离开处罚席或接受个人处罚时，处罚期满的

第六章 旱地冰球竞赛规则
Chapter Six The Rules for Game

of penalties for his team makes this impossible or the penalty expiring is a personal penalty. A goalkeeper, whose penalty expires, shall not leave the penalty bench until the next interruption.

If a penalized player enters the rink during play, this is considered sabotage of the game.

18) When a player commits repeated offences leading to a free-hit(923).

This includes both shorter and longer time.

19) When a team systematically disrupts play by committing repeated offences leading to a free-hit (923).

This also includes when a team commits a number of minor offences during a short time. The player committing the last offence shall serve the penalty.

20) When a player intentionally delays play(924).

队员不得离开处罚席。守门员处罚期满应在下一次比赛中断才能够回到场地。

如受罚队员在比赛进行时进入场地,被认为是蓄意干扰比赛。

18) 队员重复导致任意球的犯规时(923)。

包括短时和长时犯规。

19) 当球队有计划地重复可导致任意球的犯规时(923)。

包括一队在短时间内连续小的犯规动作,最后一个犯规队员应受到处罚。

20) 球员故意延误比赛(924)。

· 249 ·

This includes when a player of the offending team is striking or taking the ball away when play is interrupted, intentionally blocking the ball against the board or a goal or intentionally damaging the ball.

21)When a team systematically delays play (924).

If the referees consider a team close to being penalized for delaying play, the team captain shall, if possible, be notified before any action is taken. The team captain shall choose a field player, who is not already penalized, to serve the penalty. This also applies when a player of the defending team intentionally moves the goal cage.

22)When a player or a member of the team staff protests against the referees'decisions, or when coaching is performed in a disturbing or otherwise incorrect way (925).

这包括进攻队球员在比赛中断时将球打开或踢开，故意将球扔向挡板、球门或故意损坏球。

21）球队有计划的延误比赛（924）。

如果裁判认为球队有类似因拖延比赛而受罚行为，需在判罚前警告该队队长。队长应选择一名未受罚的队员来接受处罚。此判罚也适用于防守方队员有意移走球门。

22）当队员或球队成员向裁判的决定提出抗议，或者以不冷静的方式进行指导时（925）。

第六章 旱地冰球竞赛规则
Chapter Six The Rules for Game

This includes when the team captain constantly and without reason questions the referees' decisions.

Protesting against the referees' decisions and coaching in a disturbing way is considered spontaneous and a minor offence compared to unsportsmanlike behaviour.

This also applies if a member of the team staff enters the rink without the referees' permission. The referee shall, if possible, notify the team staff before any action is taken.

23) When a goalkeeper, despite summons from the referees, omits to put the goal cage back into position (925).

It is the goalkeeper's responsibility to put the goal cage back as soon as this is considered possible.

24) When a player, despite summons from the referees, omits to correct his personal equipment (no offence sign).

包括队长持续无理由地质疑裁判的判罚。

抗议裁判或以不冷静方式现场指导被认为不合乎体育精神，判犯规。

也包括当某球队成员未经裁判许可进入比赛场地，如果可能，裁判应在采取判罚动作之前先予以警告。

23) 当守门员无视裁判的要求，拒绝将球门恢复原位 (925)。

守门员有义务尽快努力将球门复原。

24) 队员没有按裁判要求处理自己的装备（无犯规标志）。

·251·

25)When a player uses incorrect clothing (no offence sign).

Offences concerning clothing shall only lead to one penalty per team per match. All other instances of incorrect equipment such as team captain's armlet or missing chest figures shall be reported to the administrating authority. The referee shall, if possible, notify the player before any action is taken.

26)When a goalkeeper participates in play improperly equipped(no offence sign).

If the goalkeeper unintentionally loses his face mask, play shall be interrupted and resumed with a face-off.

27) When a player deliberately prevents a goal or a goal scoring situation by committing an offence which is normally punished with a free-hit (no offence sign).

25) 队员穿着不正确的球衣（无犯规标志）。

球衣不正确，每场比赛只能判某队一次犯规，其他装备的错误如队长袖标、号码脱落等需要向主管方报告，裁判在可能情况下，判罚前应当先给予警告。

26) 当守门员在比赛中使用不正确的装备（无犯规标志）。

如果守门员无意中将面具脱落，则中断比赛，并从争球重新开始。

27) 当队员故意犯规阻止进球得分或破坏射门时，通常情况下可判罚任意球（无犯规标志）。

第六章　旱地冰球竞赛规则

Chapter Six　The Rules for Game

606 5 minute bench penalty

If the opposing team scores during a 5 minute bench penalty, the penalty shall not terminate.

If a 5 minute bench penalty is imposed in connection with a penalty shot or a delayed penalty shot, the rules concerning penalties in connection with a penalty shot shall also be applied.

607 Offences leading to a 5 minute bench penalty

1)When a field player, performs violent or dangerous strikes with his stick (901).

This includes when a field player raises his stick over an opponent's head and the opponent is hit.

2)When a field player uses his stick to hook an opponent's body (906).

3)When a player throws his

606 5分钟退场处罚

如果犯规方在5分钟退场处罚期间得分，5分钟退场处罚不会因此结束。

如果因罚点球或推迟罚点球而致5分钟退场处罚，则犯规引起的罚点球规则适用。

607 导致5分钟退场处罚的犯规

1) 场员用球杆作出暴力或危险动作时（901）。

包括将球杆举过对手头顶且对方受击。

2) 场员用球杆钩对方身体（906）。

3) 队员掷其球杆或其他

stick or other equipment on the rink to hit or try to hit the ball (909).

4)When a player throws himself towards an opponent or otherwise attacks an opponent violently (909).

5)When a player tackles, throws or trips an opponent against the board or the goal cage(909).

6)When a player commits repeated offences, each leading to a 2 minute bench penalty (923).

The 5 minute bench penalty replaces the last 2 minute bench penalty. The offences shall be similar.

608 Personal penalty

1)A personal penalty can only be imposed in connection with a bench penalty and shall not be measured until the bench penalty expires or terminates. An unlimited number of personal penalties may be measured simultaneously.

装备击球或尝试击球（909）。

4）队员以身体强烈的冲击和碰撞对手（909）。

5）队员将对手推或铲至挡板及球门（909）。

6）球员反复犯规，每次犯规均可导致2分钟退场处罚时（923）。

5分钟退场犯规可替代最后一次2分钟退场犯规，前提是犯规内容相似。

608 个人处罚

1）个人处罚只可与退场处罚相关联，且退场处罚执行结束之后方可执行。可以同时执行若干个人处罚。

第六章　旱地冰球竞赛规则
Chapter Six　The Rules for Game

If a player, already serving a personal penalty, incurs a bench penalty, the measuring of the remaining personal penalty shall, as soon as the bench penalty can be measured, be postponed until the bench penalty expires or terminates. The team captain shall choose a field player, who is not already penalized, to accompany the player on the penalty bench in order to enter the rink when the bench penalty expires.

2)A personal penalty shall only affect the player, and due to this he may be replaced on the rink during the penalty.

The team captain shall choose a field player, who is not already penalized, to accompany the player on the penalty bench in order to enter the rink when the bench penalty expires.

Only the penalized player shall be noted in the match record. When the personal penalty expires, the player shall

如果队员已受个人处罚，又犯规导致退场处罚，可先执行退场处罚，剩余的个人处罚应当延迟至退场处罚结束或终止时执行，队长可以选择一名未受处罚的场员陪受罚者坐在处罚席上，以便受罚队员处罚结束后尽快回到比赛。

2) 个人惩罚只影响球员，因此处罚期间他在场地内可被更换。

队长可以选择一名未受处罚的场员陪受罚者坐在处罚席上，以便处罚结束时受罚队员尽快回到比赛。

处罚球员应当在记录中标明。当个人处罚期满后队员只能在比赛中断时回到场内。

not enter the rink until play is interrupted.

The referees shall, together with the secretariat, help a player, whose personal penalty has expired during play, to leave the penalty bench as soon as play is interrupted. A member of the team staff incurring a personal penalty shall be sent to the spectators' stand for the rest of the match, and the team captain shall choose a field player, who is not already penalized, to serve the bench penalty.

609 10 minute personal penalty

If the opposing team scores during a 10 minute personal penalty, the penalty shall not terminate.

610 Offences leading to a 2 minute bench penalty + 10 minute personal penalty

When a player or a member of the team staff is guilty of

裁判应与记录员一同帮助处罚期满的队员在比赛中断时及时回到赛场。球队工作人员受到个人处罚后，比赛结束前只能去观众席。同时队长应选择一名未受罚队员接受这次处罚。

609 10分钟退场处罚

如犯规方在10分钟退场处罚期间得分，该处罚不可中止。

610 导致2分钟退场处罚加10分钟退场处罚的犯规

队员或球队工作人员违背体育精神的不冷静行为

Chapter Six The Rules for Game

unsportsmanlike behaviour (925).

Unsportsmanlike behaviour implies: behaving in an insulting or unfair way towards referees, players, team staff, officials, spectators, or any simulating action intended to deceive the referees. Intentionally kicking, upsetting or hitting the board or the goal cage. Throwing the stick or any other equipment, even during an interruption or in the substitution zone.

611 Match penalty

1) A player or a member of the team staff incurring a match penalty shall immediately go to the dressing room and must not take any further part in the match.

The organiser is responsible for ensuring that the offender goes to the dressing room and does not return to the spectators' stand or the rink during the remaining time of the match, possible extra time and

（925）。

有违体育精神行为即以侮辱或不正当方式攻击裁判、对手、对方工作人员、官员、记录员或采取过激行为欺骗裁判。故意踢打挡板、球门。投掷球杆及其他装备，即使在比赛中断或在休息区时也如此。

611 罚离场

1）队员或球队工作人员被判罚离场时应立刻去更衣室，且不得参与任何剩余比赛。

主办方应确认受罚者去更衣室，在比赛剩余时间内，不停留在观众席或场地附近。包括在延长赛和点球决胜阶段，所有的罚离场都需报告。

penalty shots included. All match penalties shall be reported.

A player or member of the team staff shall incur only one match penalty per match with exception from a match penalty when not noted in the match record. Subsequent offences leading to a match penalty shall be reported, but no further bench penalty shall be imposed with exception from a match penalty incurred for a player or member of team staff not noted in the match record.

Offences committed before or after the match, which normally lead to a match penalty, shall be reported, but no bench penalty shall be imposed. With the exception of incorrect equipment (which shall be corrected by the player concerned, who may then start the match), offences leading to a match penalty committed before the match shall also lead to the offender's non participation in the match,

一名队员或球队工作人员一场比赛只能被罚离场一次，除非记录上没有罚离场记录。导致罚离场的犯规应当被记录，罚离场后不得追加其他的退场处罚，除非队员或球队成员的被罚离场没有记录在案。

赛前或赛后的犯规行为通常会导致罚离场，需要被报告，但不必追加退场处罚。不正确的设备除外(予以校正后方可在这场比赛中首发上场)，赛前犯规导致被罚离场，该球员不得参加本场比赛，可能的加时赛和点球战也包括在内。

第六章　旱地冰球竞赛规则

Chapter Six　The Rules for Game

possible extra time and penalty shots included.

2) A match penalty shall always be followed by a 5 minute bench penalty.

The team captain shall choose a field player, who is not already penalized, to serve the bench penalty, and possible other bench penalties concerning the player or member of the team staff incurring the match penalty. Only the penalized player shall be noted in the match record. Possible personal penalties concerning the player incurring a match penalty shall terminate. If a player having received a match penalty makes a further offence leading to a match penalty, the offence leading to a severer match penalty will be noted in the match record.

612 Match penalty 1

Match penalty 1 shall lead to suspension for the rest of the match and shall not lead to any further punishment for the player.

2) 罚离场一般还有5分钟退场处罚。

当队员或球队成员引发罚离场处罚时，该队队长须在未受罚队员中选择一名接受退场处罚，也有可能其他退场处罚的队员或球队成员招致了罚离场。只有被罚队员应当在记录纸上注明，也有可能个人处罚者招致被罚离场时，个人处罚终止。如果一名已受到罚离场处罚的队员继续犯规导致再次被判罚离场，该犯规导致严重被罚离场，应被记录在案。

612 第一类罚离场

第一类罚离场导致队员无法参加剩余比赛，且不追加其他判罚。

·259·

613 Offences leading to a match penalty 1

1)When a field player uses a non-approved stick, a stick consisting of a blade and a shaft of two different brands or a stick with a hook which is too wide.

When a goalkeeper uses an incorrect face mask (no offence sign).

A stick without approval mark is always considered to be non-approved.

2)When a player or a member of the team staff, not noted in the match record, participates in the match (no offence sign).

3)When an injured player, who has been replaced on the penalty bench, participates in play before his penalty time has expired (no offence sign).

4)When a player is guilty of continued or repeated unsportsmanlike behaviour (925).

613 导致第一类罚离场的犯规

1) 当队员使用未经认证不合规格的球杆，球杆和杆头为不同品牌，或球杆弯钩太宽。

守门员使用未经认证的面具（无犯规标志）。

无认证标志的球杆为不合格。

2) 没报名的队员或球队工作人员参与了比赛（无犯规标志）。

3) 被替换的受伤退场的受罚队员在处罚时间结束前参与了比赛。

4)当球员反复持续进行有违体育精神的行为（925）。

第六章　旱地冰球竞赛规则
Chapter Six   The Rules for Game

The match penalty replaces the second 2 minute bench penalty + 10 minute personal penalty, but shall still be followed by a 5 minute bench penalty. Continued implies in the same sequence and repeated for the second time in the same match.

5)When a player, in anger, breaks his stick or other equipment (925).

6)When a player is guilty of dangerous physical play (909).

This includes dangerous, violent or unsportsmanlike offences considered deliberate or unprovoked.

614 Match penalty 2

Match penalty 2 shall also lead to suspension from the following match in the same competition.

615 Offences leading to a match penalty 2

1)When a player or a member of the team staff participates in a scuffle (909).

罚离场可以代替第二次2分钟退场处罚加10分钟个人处罚，但是仍要有5分钟退场处罚随后。持续意味着在同一场比赛中以同样顺序重复了第二次。

5）队员因愤怒损坏其球杆或其他设备（925）。

6）队员进行危险的身体对抗行为（909）。

包括故意或无被激怒情况下的危险、暴力、有违运动员道德的动作。

614 第二类罚离场

第二类罚离场也会导致无法参加剩余的比赛。

615 导致第二类罚离场的犯规

1）当队员或球队工作人员参与混战（909）。

A scuffle implies a milder form of a fight, without punches or kicks, where the players involved respect attempts to separate them.

2)When a player commits an offence leading to a 5 minute bench penalty, for the second time in the same match (923).

The match penalty replaces the second 5 minute bench penalty, but shall still be followed by a 5 minute bench penalty.

3)When a member of the team staff, is guilty of continued or repeated unsportsmanlike behaviour (925).

The match penalty replaces the second 2 minute bench penalty+10 minute personal penalty, but shall still be followed by a 5 minute bench penalty.

4)When a player, whose equipment is about to be controlled, tries to correct or exchange the equipment before the control of the equipment (925).

混战意味着在相对温和的对抗局面下，没有拳打脚踢，队员应试图将参加人员分开。

2) 队员在一场比赛中第二次犯规导致5分钟退场处罚（923）。

罚离场替代了第二次5分钟退场处罚，但是还应追加处罚5分钟退场。

3) 当球队工作人员持续反复地有违运动员道德的行为（925）。

罚离场可以代替第二次2分钟退场处罚加10分钟个人处罚，但仍应追加5分钟退场处罚。

4) 当其设备被没收之前，运动员试图纠正、更换设备（925）。

第六章　旱地冰球竞赛规则
Chapter Six　The Rules for Game

5) When a player or a member of the team staff commits an offence clearly intending to sabotage play (925).

This includes when:

A penalized player intentionally enters the rink during play, before his penalty expires or terminates. If the rink is entered during an interruption in play a 2 minute bench penalty shall be imposed. If the secretariat is responsible for a player being admitted to the rink too soon, and the mistake is noticed during regular penalty time, the player shall resume his position on the penalty bench. There shall not be any additional penalty time and the player shall return to the rink when his regular penalty time expires. If the mistake is noticed after the regular penalty time has expired, no action shall be taken. If a player, whose penalty has expired, enters the rink despite the numeric situation does

5）当队员或球队工作人员显然蓄意破坏比赛进程（925）。

包括：

受罚队员在处罚期满前故意进入比赛场地。如果比赛中断时进入场地，应处以2分钟退场处罚。如果记录台过早让队员回到赛场，且该过错在正规处罚期内被发现，则该队员须回到处罚席继续受罚；不再附加其他处罚时间，场员处罚时间结束后应回到场地。若该过错在常规受罚时间结束后发现，则不该有任何附加处罚。球员在处罚时间结束后，必须等待比赛中断方可返回比赛，否则可能被视为队员过多的状况。

request him to wait for the next interruption, it can, depending on its cause, be considered to be 'playing with too many players'.

Offences are committed by either team from the substitution zone, during a penalty shot.

Equipment is thrown from the substitution zone during play.

A player, not in the process of changing, takes part or tries to take part in play from the substitution zone.

A player participates as a field player after having participated as a goal keeper in the same game.

A team intentionally has too many players on the rink.

6) When a field player continues to use a defective stick or uses a strengthened or lengthened shaft (no offence sign).

在罚点球期间来自休息区的任何犯规行为。

比赛进行中从休息区掷出的任何装备。

非换人过程中的球员从休息区参与或试图参与比赛。

在当过守门员之后又成为场员。

球队故意有过多队员参与比赛。

6) 场员继续使用不合规则的球杆，包括加长或加粗的球杆（无犯规标志）。

第六章　旱地冰球竞赛规则　
Chapter Six　The Rules for Game

616 Match penalty 3

Match penalty 3 shall also lead to suspension from the following match in the same competition, and further punishment decided by the administrating authority.

617 Offences leading to a match penalty 3

1) When a player or a member of the team staff is involved in a fight (909).

A player is considered to be involved in a fight when he uses punches or kicks.

2) When a player or a member of the team staff is guilty of a brutal offence(909).

This also includes throwing a stick or other equipment at an opponent.

3) When a player or a member of the team staff is guilty of rude misconduct (925).

Rude misconduct implies

616 第三类罚离场

第三类罚离场也会导致队员无法参加剩余比赛，且主管办方可视情况追加处罚。

617 可导致第三类罚离场的犯规

1) 当一名队员或者球队工作人员参与了打斗（909）。

队员使用拳击或者脚踢就被认为是参与了打斗。

2) 当一名队员或者球队工作人员使用了过度的带有伤害性质的暴力行为（909）。

包括将球杆及其他装备掷向对方。

3) 当一名队员或者工作人员采用了粗鲁无礼的行动（925）。

例如侮辱了裁判员、球

•265•

grossly insulting referees, players, team staff, officials or spectators.

4)When a player or a member of the team staff is guilty of violent conduct.

Violent conduct means a deliberate impact on the physical integrity of a person without causing injury.

618 Penalties in connection with a penalty shot

1)If a penalty shot results in a goal, the penalty causing the penalty, if it is a 2 minute bench penalty, shall be terminated.

This includes a delayed penalty shot.

2)If during a delayed penalty shot, the offending team commits another offence leading to a penalty shot, the second offence shall be considered the offence causing the penalty shot. If a penalty shot is interrupted due to an offence caused by the

员、球队工作人员、官员或观众。

4) 当一名队员或者球队工作人员使用了暴力动作。

暴力动作是指虽无受伤但可能造成对方身体不适的行动。

618 关于罚点球的犯规

1) 如果罚球得分，则正在进行的2分钟罚退场应结束，包括推迟的罚点球。

2) 如果推迟罚点球期间犯规队又有导致罚球的犯规，则第二次犯规应被视为引发了罚点球。如果罚点球是由于守门员的犯规，则守门员的犯规应被视为引发了新的罚球。如果在一个5分

第六章　旱地冰球竞赛规则
Chapter Six　The Rules for Game

goalkeeper, the goalkeeper's offence shall be considered the cause of the new penalty shot. If a 5 minute bench penalty is imposed in connection with a penalty shot or a delayed penalty shot an already existing 2 minute bench penalty shall be terminated if the penalty shot results in a goal.

钟退场犯规期间发生了2分钟退场犯规并引发了罚点球并射门得分，则这个2分钟退场犯规不须执行。

Section Seven: Goals

701 Allowed goals

1)A goal shall be considered allowed when it has been correctly scored and confirmed with a face-off at the centre spot.

All allowed goals shall be noted in the match record with the time and the numbers of the scoring and assisting players. As assisting player is considered a player of the same team directly involved in the scoring. Only one assist per goal shall be noted. A goal scored during extra time or from a penalty shot after a period or a match has ended shall not

第七节　得分

701 合法得分

1) 当球被合法的打进球门之后，被认为是合法得分，同时应从中心点争球。

所有的合法进球的时间、数目、射门球员以及助攻球员都必须比赛记录上注明。助攻球员是直接影响射门的人员。每次进球只需记录一名助攻球员，加时赛或者罚球时的进球不需要经过争球进行，但如果两名裁判都指向中心点和球门，并且进球已经记录时允许争球进行。

be confirmed with a face-off, but shall be considered allowed when both referees have pointed at the centre spot and the goal has been noted in the match record.

2)An allowed goal must not be disallowed after the face-off is made.

If the referees are certain that an allowed goal is incorrect, this shall be reported.

702 Correctly scored goals

1)When the entire ball passes the goal line from the front, having been played in a correct way with a field player's stick, and no offence leading to a free-hit or a penalty has been committed by the attacking team in connection with, or immediately before, the goal.

This includes:

When a player in the defending team has moved the goal cage out of position and the ball passes the goal line from the

2) 场中争球后所有已获得分不得被修改。

如果裁判坚持已获得分不正确，此事应报告给赛会。

702 正确进球得分

1) 当球从前方穿过球门线，由场上球员正确击出，在没有犯规导致任意球，攻击方在击球过程前后也没有犯规动作的情况下，此球为正确进球。

这包括：

防守队员移动了球门的位置，球从杆的下方和原先的位置标记之间从前面穿过

第六章　旱地冰球竞赛规则
Chapter Six　The Rules for Game

front between the marks for the posts and below the imaginary position of the bar.

When an own goal is scored. An own goal may be allowed off the stick or body of the defender. If the non-offending team scores an own goal during a delayed penalty, the goal shall be allowed.

An own goal shall be noted as OG.

2) When the entire ball passes the goal line from the front after a player in the defending team has directed the ball with his stick or his body, or a player in the attacking team has unintentionally directed the ball with his body, and no offence leading to a free-hit or a penalty has been committed by the attacking team in connection with, or immediately before the goal.

The goal shall not be considered correctly scored if a field player in the attacking team intentionally kicks the ball immediately before it is directed

球门线。

当打了乌龙球时，它可以远离球杆或防守者。如果未违规的一方在延迟处罚中得分，此得分应予以被承认。

自身的进球应被记为乌龙球（Own Goal）。

2) 当防守球员用自己的球杆或身体控球，进攻队员无意识地用身体控球，在进球过程中进攻队员没有犯规行为也没有由犯规所引起的任意球，在这种情况下，球从前方进入穿过球门线也被记为正确进球。

如进攻队有意射门前踢球，进球无效。如果队员不正确运杆而射门得分，球过

•269•

into goal. If a player has scored with an incorrect stick and the mistake is noticed only after the ball has passed the goal line, the goal shall be allowed.

3) When a player who is not noted in the match record, or is incorrectly numbered, is involved in the scoring of a goal.

Involved implies scoring or assisting.

703 Incorrect scored goals

1) When a player in the attacking team has committed an offence leading to a free-hit or a penalty in connection with, or immediately before, the goal (prescribed offence sign).

This includes when a team scores with too many players or a penalized player on the rink, and when a player in the attacking team intentionally moves the goal cage out of position.

2) When a player in the attacking team intentionally

了球门线才指出错误，得分有效。

3) 当球员没有被计入比赛记录，或者号码有误，其所参与射门有效。

参与进球得分包括进球和协助进球。

703 不合法进球

1) 当进攻队队员在射门前或者射门时已有可判罚任意球或罚球的犯规行为（需要鸣犯规哨）。

这包括当球队有太多球员在场上、被处罚的球员在场或进攻队队员故意移动球门而致。

2) 当一个进攻球员故意用身体将球顶进球门。

第六章　旱地冰球竞赛规则
Chapter Six　The Rules for Game

directs the ball into goal with any part of his body.

Since this is not considered an offence, play shall be resumed with a face-off.

3) When the ball passes the goal line during, or after, a signal.

A period or a match is over as soon as the final signal has started sounding.

4) When the ball goes into the goal cage witthout passing the goal line from the front.

5) When a goalkeeper throws or kicks the ball into the opposing team's goal, in an otherwise correct way.

Since this is not considered an offence, play shall be resumed with a face-off. The ball has to touch another player or another player's equipment before it goes into goal.

6) When a field player in the attacking team intentionally kicks the ball and it goes into goal after

这不被认为是一次进攻，应重新争球。

3）当球在哨声响起时或之后进入球门。

比赛或者某一阶段在结束哨声响起时，立即结束。

4）当球部分进入球门，却没有完全穿越球门线前端。

5）当一个守门员将球扔或踢进对手的球门，或者以另外的合理的方式。

由于这不被认为是进攻，应重新争球。球在进门前必须接触其他队员或其装备。

6）当一名场员有意将球踢向其他队员或其装备导致进球。

·271·

having touched another player or another player's equipment.

Since this is not considered an offence, play shall be resumed with a face-off.

7) When the offending team scores during a delayed penalty.

The penalty shall be carried out and play resumed with a face-off.

8) When the ball bounces off one of the referees and directly into goal.

这不被认为是一次进攻，比赛应重新争球。

7) 当犯规队在延迟处罚中射门得分，应执行处罚，重新争球。

8) 当球打在裁判身上折射入球门。

第六章　旱地冰球竞赛规则
Chapter Six　The Rules for Game

Section Eight: Consequence Signs

第八节　裁判手势

801 Stoppage of game time/time out

801 比赛时间结束/比赛暂停

The fingertips held perpendicular to the palm of the hand.

手指指尖举起与另一手手掌垂直。

802 Face-off

802 争球

The fore-arms held horizontally, the palms of the hands downwards.

两前臂平行举起，掌心向下。

•273•

北欧时尚运动——旱地冰球
Nordic Fashion Sport FLOORBALL

803 Hit-in

The arm held horizontally in the advantage direction, the palm of the hand downwards.

803 边线球

一只手臂水平指向球权方，掌心向下。

804 Free-hit

The arm held horizontally, in the advantage direction, the palm of the hand downwards.

804 任意球

一只手臂水平指向球权方，掌心向下。

中国旱地冰球信息网 www.floorballinfo.com
国际旱地冰球联合会 www.floorball.org

第六章　旱地冰球竞赛规则　

Chapter Six　The Rules for Game

805 Advantage　　805 球权

The arm held in the advantage direction, the palm of the hand upwards.

胳膊指向球权方，掌心向上。

806 Penalty shot　　806 罚点球

北欧时尚运动——旱地冰球
Nordic Fashion Sport FLOORBALL

807 Delayed penalty/ Delayed penalty shot
807 延迟处罚/延迟罚点球

The arm held vertically, the palm of the hand forwards.

胳膊向上垂直举起，掌心向前。

808 Bench penalty/ Personal penalty
808 退场处罚/个人处罚

The arm held vertically, the number of minutes shown with the fingers, 10 minutes with a clenched hand.

胳膊向上垂直举起，伸出的手指数目代表处罚时间，手握拳代表处罚10分钟。

第六章 旱地冰球竞赛规则
Chapter Six   The Rules for Game

809 Match penalty

The arm held vertically.

809 罚离场

胳膊向上垂直举起。

810 Goal

The arm in the direction of first the goal and then the centre shot, the palm of the hand downwards.

810 得分

胳膊首先指向球门，然后指向中心点，掌心向下。

811 Continue play/ Incorrectly scored goal

The arm held horizontally, the palm of the hands downwards.

811 比赛继续/不合法进球

两胳膊平举,掌心向下。

Section Nine: Offence Signs

第九节 犯规手势

901 Incorrectly hit

One blow with the hand.

901 非正确击球

手掌击一下前臂。

第六章　旱地冰球竞赛规则
Chapter Six　The Rules for Game

902　Locking an opponent's stick

The palms of hands downwards.

902　压住对手球杆

两掌心交叉下压。

903　Lifting an opponent's stick

The palm of the hands downwards.

903　抬起对手球杆

掌心向下。

北欧时尚运动——旱地冰球
Nordic Fashion Sport FLOORBALL

904 High stick
904 高杆

Imitating the holding of a stick.　　做出举杆的动作。

905 Placing stick, foot or leg between an opponent's legs
905 将球杆、脚或腿放在对手两腿之间

第六章　旱地冰球竞赛规则
Chapter Six　The Rules for Game

906 Hooking

The forearms held horizontally, imitating the holding of a stick.

906 勾住对方

前臂平行弯曲，做拿杆的动作。

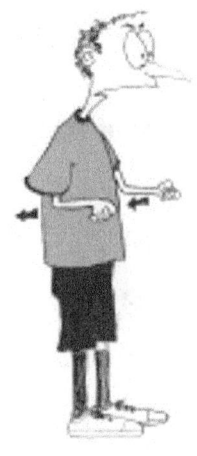

907 Incorrectly pushing

Can be performed with only one hand.

907 不正确推人

也可以使用单手。

北欧时尚运动——旱地冰球
Nordic Fashion Sport FLOORBALL

908 Backing into an opponent

908 后背撞人

The hands cupped, the palms of the hands upwards, the forearms pulled backwards.

手掌微弯，掌心向上，小臂做向后拉的动作。

909 Roughing

909 暴躁

The backs of the hands upwards.

两手相抵，手背朝上。

第六章　旱地冰球竞赛规则
Chapter Six　The Rules for Game

910 Holding 910 拉人

911 Interference 911 干扰

北欧时尚运动——旱地冰球
Nordic Fashion Sport FLOORBALL

912 Incorrect kick

The foot turned outwards, on a level with the ankle.

912 不当踢球

脚向上抬起，与脚踝在同一水平。

913 High kick

The foot turned outwards, on a level with the knee.

913 高踢腿

脚向上抬起，与膝盖在同一水平。

第六章　旱地冰球竞赛规则
Chapter Six　The Rules for Game

914 Entering the goalkeeper area

914 进入守门员区域

915 Incorrect distance

915 不当距离

The forearms held vertically.

前臂垂直，手心相对。

916 Incorrect jump   916 不当跳起

The palms of the hands upwards.   两手掌心向上。

917 Incorrect throw-out   917 不当抛球

The forearms held horizontally, the palms of the hands facing each other.

前臂弯曲平行，掌心相对。

第六章　旱地冰球竞赛规则
Chapter Six　The Rules for Game

918 Incorrect hit-in/ Incorrect free-hit

918 错误边线球/错误任意球

The palm of the hand upwards, in the direction of the original hit-in /freehit.

掌心向上，指向原来的边线球/任意球方向。

919 Playing the ball lying down

919 躺下击球

The palm of the hand downwards.

左手下垂于腿侧，右手掌心向下，身前平扫过。

•287•

北欧时尚运动——旱地冰球
Nordic Fashion Sport FLOORBALL

920 Hands

The palm of the right hand upwards.

920 手球

右手掌心向上。

921 Header

The palm of the hand to the forehead.

921 头球

右手掌心摸向额头。

第六章　旱地冰球竞赛规则
Chapter Six　The Rules for Game

922 Incorrect substitution　　922 不当换人

The forearms rotating.　　转动前臂。

923 Repeated offences　　923 重复犯规

Three blows with the hand.　　手掌垂直击打前臂三下。

•289•

北欧时尚运动——旱地冰球
Nordic Fashion Sport FLOORBALL

924 Delaying play   924 延迟

925 Misconduct   925 错误行为

第六章 旱地冰球竞赛规则
Chapter Six The Rules for Game

第十节 场地规格
Section Ten: Illustration of the Rink

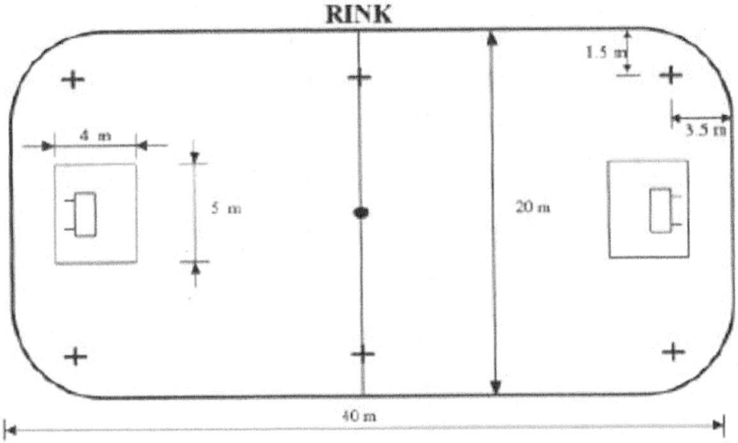

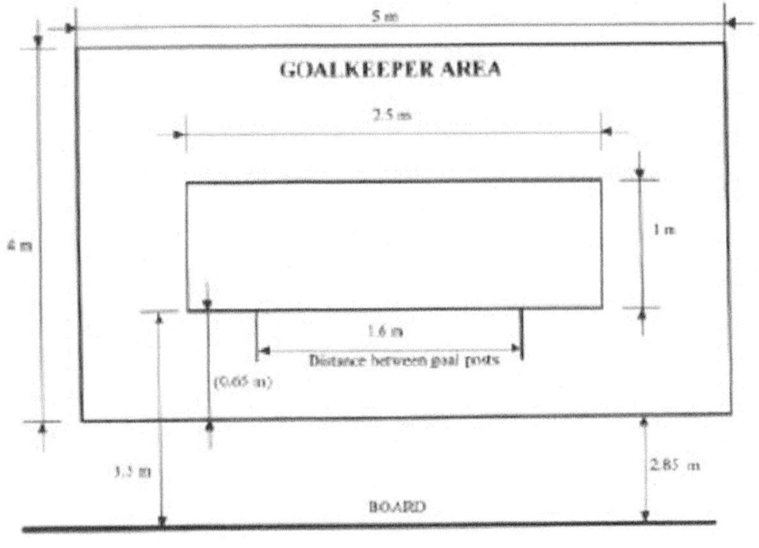

附 录
专业旱地冰球运动词汇汉英对照表
Appendix
Vocabulary of Professional Floorball Terms in Chinese & English

Floorball ['flɔ: bɔ:l] 音译福乐球，中国称旱地冰球、地面球（非正式）

Stick [stik] 球杆

Shaft [ʃɑ:ft, ʃæft] （球杆）手柄

Blade [bleid] （球杆）击球板

SFF（Swedish Floorball Federation）瑞典旱地冰球联盟

IFF（International Floorball Federation）国际旱地冰球联合会

GAISF（General Association of International Sports Federation）国际单项体育联合会总会

FISU（International University Sports Federation）世界大学生运动联合会

EMSA（E-Sports Management Australia）澳大利亚电子竞技管理局

Penetration [,peni'treiʃən] 参与度

Invasion [in,veiʒən] 进攻性的

Stance [stɑ:ns, stæns] 站位

Forehand ['fɔ:hænd] 正手

Cushion ['kuʃən] 缓冲

Aerial ['eəriəl] 高（球）

Backswing ['bæk,swiŋ] （球拍的）向后挥拍

Dribble ['dribl] 运球

Backhand ['bæk'hænd] 反手

Fake [feik] 假动作

Transition [træn'ziʃən, -'si-] 快攻

Counter attack 反攻

Defense [di'fens] 防守

Offence [ə'fens] 进攻、犯规

Goalkeeper ['gəul,ki:pə] 守门员

Free-hit 任意球

Penalty shot 点球

Face-off 争球

Hit-in 界外球

GBFUA (Great Britain Floorball & Unihockey Association) 英国旱地冰球及冰球协会

FFF （Finland Floorball Federation）芬兰旱地冰球联合会

Middle line 中线

Power play 以多打少

EFC（Euro Floorball Cup）旱地冰球欧洲杯

Tactic ['tæktik] 战术，策略

Street Floorball 街头旱地冰球

Swamp Floorball 沼泽旱地冰球

Sand Floorball 沙地旱地冰球

Rink [riŋk] 球场，场地

Participation [pɑːˌtisi'peiʃən] 参赛人员

Fixed situation 定位球

Penalty ['penlti] 处罚

Consequence ['kɔnsikwəns] 裁判

中国旱地冰球信息网 www.floorballinfo.com
国际旱地冰球联合会 www.floorball.org

参考资料及来源
References or Sources

1. IFF Material

IFF资料

(Some of them are from IFF official website: www.floorball.org)

（其中部分资料来自IFF官方网站：www.floorball.org）

2. Material from the IFF Member Federations

IFF会员资料

3. *Learn Start Play*

《入门玩法》

4. *Youth Startup Kit*

《青年入门装备》

中国旱地冰球信息网 www.floorballinfo.com
国际旱地冰球联合会 www.floorball.org

References & Authors 参考书目和作者

- **Learn Start Play**

This material has been created by AnniinaPaavilainen, Emily Koh, MeritaBruun and John Liljelund and edited by MeritaBruun and John Liljelund.

Emily Koh

A teacher and a national team player, Singapore

AnniinaPaavilainen

Bachelor of leisure and sports management, Finland

MeritaBruun

IFF Information Manager

John Liljelund

IFF Secretary General

- 《入门玩法》

这个素材是由Anniina-Paavilainen, Emily Koh, MeritaBruun and John Liljelund等人撰写，MeritaBruun and John Liljelund等人整理的。

Emily Koh

新加坡教练、国家队队员

AnniinaPaavilainen

芬兰休闲与运动管理学士

MeritaBruun

国际旱地冰球联合会信息管理员

John Liljelund

国际旱地冰球联合会秘书长

- **FFF (Finland Floorball Federation)**

Individual Technique and Tactics Tekniikka japerustilanteet, 1999

The education material of the Finnish Floorball Federation

Salibandynnuoriso jaaikuisvalmennus, 2006

- **Unihockey Techniques DVD**

Swiss Unihockey Association/IFF, 2006

- **Decision Training, A New Approach to Coaching**

Dr. J.N.Vickers, Faculty of Kinesio-logy and The National Coaching institute-Calgary, University of Calgary

- **Innebandytaktik**

SISU Idrot-tsböcker/Swedish Floorball-Federation, 2003

- 芬兰旱地冰球联合会素材

《个人技巧与战术》,1999 Tekniikka japerustilanteet

《青少年及成人旱地冰球培训》,2006 Salibandynnuoriso jaaikuisvalmennus

- 联合冰球技术DVD素材

瑞士联合冰球协会/国际旱地冰球协会,2006

- 《场上判断训练——新的教练之路》

J.N.Vickers博士,加拿大卡尔加里大学人体运动学学院、国家教练部卡尔加里分部

- 《旱地冰球战术》

SISU 体育图书/瑞典旱地冰球联合会,2003

• **Rules of the Game Edition 2010**

International Floorball Federation, Rules and Competition Committee

• ***Drawings: Anna Eriksson***

•《比赛规则》，2010

国际旱地冰球联合会规则与竞技委员会

• 绘图：Anna Eriksson

中国旱地冰球信息网 www.floorballinfo.com
国际旱地冰球联合会 www.floorball.org